Bay

Drainage

Atlantic Drainage

**A Guide to the Freshwater Sport Fishes
of Canada**

To Joe:
Complements of the author
Don

J Nelson

National Museum of Natural Sciences
Natural History Series, No. 1

Published by the
National Museums of Canada

A Guide to the Freshwater Sport Fishes
of Canada

D. E. McAllister
E. J. Crossman
Illustrated by C. H. Douglas

Available by mail
from the
National Museums of Canada
Marketing Services Division
Ottawa, Ontario
K1A 0M8

Catalogue No. NM 95-17/1

National Museums of Canada
Ottawa, Canada
1973

P0987654321
Y79876543
Printed in Canada

Disponible en français

Dedicated to the true sportsman

CONTENTS

LIST OF ILLUSTRATIONS

Black-and-White Plates

Colour Plates

ACKNOWLEDGEMENTS

Mr. C. G. Gruchy, Dr. C. C. Lindsey, Dr. S. U. Qadri and Mr. T. A. Willock kindly criticized the manuscript. Dr. J. G. Hunter provided information on distribution of arctic fishes as well as data on Arctic charr and Pacific salmon, Mr. C. G. Gruchy on Lake of the Woods area fishes, Mr. T. A. Willock on southern Alberta fishes. Mr. V. Legendre gave extensive information on Quebec fishes as well as considerable assistance with French-Canadian names, Dr. M. V. Atton and the late Mr. W. H. Van Vliet on Saskatchewan fish and fishing, and Mr. J.-P. Cuerrier on distribution, especially in the National Parks.

Mr. H. Haswell and Mr. Howard H. Berry gave generous assistance on fishing flies of New Brunswick, Dr. J. Hatter and Mr. G. Ferguson on those of British Columbia, and Mr. W. E. Organ on those of Manitoba. Mr. Mike Ball provided records from *Field and Stream* files; Mr. R. Pelletier of Molson Fishing Club provided data on record fishes from Quebec, and Mr. T. Yates of the Ontario Federation of Anglers and Hunters on Ontario fishes.

Dr. T. F. McCarthy gave valuable assistance in writing the section on rescue breathing; Mr. K. M. Parks provided information on boating. Miss M. Myer permitted use of recipes on cooking fish, and Dr. P. Elson and the Atlantic Salmon Association permitted publication of figures from an article in the *Atlantic Salmon Journal*.

To all these persons the authors wish to express their deep gratitude.

D. E. McAllister
and E. J. Crossman
April 30, 1969

INTRODUCTION

Aims of the Book

Canada is rich in tumbling streams and rolling rivers, and in lakes — deep and shallow, pond-like and horizon-wide. Over 25 per cent of the world's fresh water is in Canada. Its 3,852,000 square miles include 292,000 square miles of fresh water. In these waters dwell 53 species of fishes that the authors consider tempting to the angler.

The principal aim of this book is to help the angler identify the fish he has caught. The figures and brief text indicate its maximum size and describe something of its habits and the usual angling methods. Maps provide ready information on distribution. Supplementary material on making fish prints, knots, cleaning and cutting fish, and recipes is included. Other sources of information useful to the angler concerning licences and regulations, travel and maps, canoeing and boating are listed on pp. 76–77. The book is designed to be an angler's companion, of a size and ruggedness convenient for thrusting into pocket or tackle box.

The book is not intended to give extensive information on angling methods, life histories or fine details of distribution. The angler is referred to the already available sources for information on these, books such as *Freshwater Fishes of Canada,* by W. B. Scott and E. J. Crossman, and other books and periodicals, listed on pp. 72–75.

This book covers the sport fishes occurring in the fresh waters of the ten provinces and two territories of Canada. Fishes living part of their lives in the sea are included only if they are angled for in fresh water. By sport fishes we mean in general those species that are widely sought after by the angler in search of sport. Forty-three of the approximately 200 kinds of fishes known from Canadian fresh waters fall into this class. Another 10 species, such as the creek chub and tench, are included. Although not frequently sought after, they have potentialities for the expanding angler population and may be of interest to the young angler. These are treated in less detail.

While this book is written to identify sport fishes in Canada, it may be of some use in Alaska and northern continental United States. Books listed on pp. 72–74 will help identify non-sport fishes incidently caught while angling.

Before we venture further, we may answer some questions often asked. What is a fish? Is a whale a fish? A fish is a cold-blooded animal with a backbone, breathing throughout life with gills, and having its limbs, if any, in the form of fins. Even though they are superficially fish-like, whales are air-breathing mammals that lack gills, are warm-blooded, nurse their young, and possess (some) hair. Salamanders may be somewhat fish-like as they are cold-blooded and sometimes have gills, but their limbs bear digits and are not fin-like.

Format

General information on fishes of particular interest to the angler is included in the Introduction. Following this explanation of the format are sections on the Structure of Fishes, Biology, How to Identify Fishes, and Preserving Specimens. A final section is devoted to the Angler and His Environment.

Family and Species Accounts, which follows the Introduction, forms the main body of the text. As far as possible, related species are grouped on the same or opposite pages for ease of comparison. Text and map adjoin the figure, thus eliminating the need to hunt for them. A standard format, described in the following paragraphs, is used for the species accounts. Unless otherwise indicated, statements are meant to apply only to Canadian sport fishes.

Figures
Above the species accounts are detailed figures. These figures are carefully drawn from actual specimens to show the general appearance and to indicate important identifying features. All fish are depicted facing in the same direction, to facilitate comparison. Green diagonal lines indicate the identifying features listed under the heading "Differ." Less important details are omitted. Insets may show some important characters in greater detail.

Names
Below the figure are the English and French common names and the scientific name. The English common name usually follows the form used in *A List of Common and Scientific Names of Fishes from the United States and Canada,* published by the American Fisheries Society (3d ed., 1970, Baltimore, Waverly Press). The French common names were obtained with the help of Mr. Vianney Legendre of the Quebec Wildlife Service. As common names sometimes vary from place to place, it is necessary to select the most apt, accurate or commonly used. Other names commonly used are listed under "Notes" or in the index.

Some explanation of scientific names is warranted. Scientific names help surmount the problems of language and of the existence of many common names. Thus one scientific name is applied to each species and is recognizable to scientists all over the world. The scientific citation *Micropterus dolomieui* Lacépède, for the smallmouth bass, consists of three parts, the first two in italics. First is the genus, with the first letter capitalized, second the species, uncapitalized, and third the authority (name of the man who described this species).

A species is a distinct kind of animal which is usually physically distinct from and normally does not interbreed with other related species. A species may include two or more subspecies that are physically different from one another, but less so than species. Also, subspecies interbreed where their ranges come in contact. Related species are placed together in a genus, and related genera are placed together in a family. For example the smallmouth bass and largemouth bass are placed together in the black bass genus *Micropterus.* Thus species and genus names are analogous to Christian names and surnames. The black bass, sunfish and crappie genera are placed together in the sunfish family, Centrarchidae. Species is used in both the singular and plural sense. Genus is the singular of genera. Rarely two species will interbreed; the resulting progeny are called hybrids.

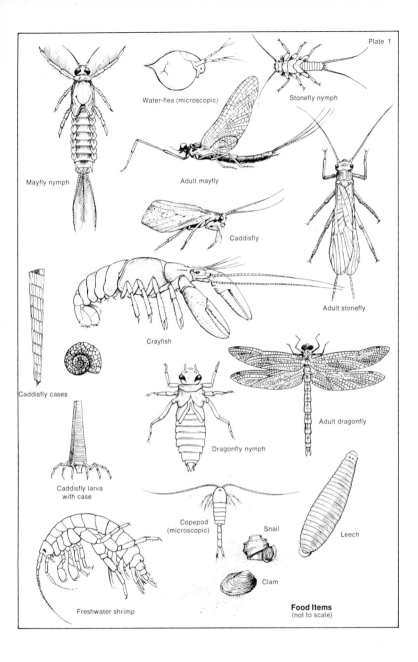

Plate 1

Water-flea (microscopic)

Stonefly nymph

Mayfly nymph

Adult mayfly

Caddisfly

Adult stonefly

Crayfish

Caddisfly cases

Caddisfly larva
with case

Dragonfly nymph

Adult dragonfly

Copepod
(microscopic)

Snail

Clam

Leech

Freshwater shrimp

Food Items
(not to scale)

Differ

Here are described the identifying features of the species, that is, how they differ from related species of Canadian freshwater sport fishes. These features are indicated on the figure above by the green diagonal lines. The features are usually listed in order, from the tip of the head tailwards. The key features will not apply in areas outside Canada because of the presence of additional species, although they may be of some use in the northern states of continental United States and in Alaska. Also they will not identify non-sport species. For identification of the latter, see books listed at the end of this guide.

Maps

The solid green areas on the maps indicate the known native distribution of the species. Green diagonal hatching indicates areas into which a species has been introduced.

The geographical distribution shown on the maps for Canadian regions is based on information in a recent and very complete Canadian study. Unfortunately no comparable study exists for United States distribution, so that we have had to draw on many scattered sources for our information on that country.

Size

The length in inches and the size in pounds and ounces are given here. The largest specimen caught by any means (including netting), the world angling record, and the largest Canadian specimen caught are included when available and as far as are known to the authors. Sometimes these categories coincide. Records kept by *Rod & Gun in Canada, Field and Stream, Molson Fishing Contests,* and the *Manitoba Master Angler Award Winners* were useful here.

Notes

Under "Notes" are given a capsule life history — habitat, food, spawning time and place, interesting features, angling methods and qualities; and sometimes books devoted solely to the species are cited. These apply to Canadian waters. Only the more frequent food items are mentioned. Plate 1 depicts some of the lesser-known invertebrate food items consumed by fishes. For reasons of brevity and function, little detail is given in this section and only the usual situation is mentioned. For further information the reader is referred to books listed at the end of the guide.

Following the Family and Species Accounts are sections on Making Fish Prints, Knots, Preparing Fish, and Rescue Breathing (or artificial respiration). Under Information Useful to the Angler are included lists of Books and Periodicals on Fishes and Anglers' Associations, as well as material on Fishing Licences and Regulations, Travel and Maps, Canoeing and Boating. A Glossary of Fish Anatomy, a Bilingual Canadian Fishing Lexicon, an index and a set of colour plates complete the volume.

Structure of Fishes

A little knowledge of the structure of fishes will add to the pleasure of examining the catch and increase one's accuracy in identifying the fish. This section provides an introduction to fish anatomy. *See* pls. 2, 3 and 4.

A fish consists of two parts, the head and the body, there being no neck. On the head are the jaws, snout, nostrils and eyes. On the snout or chin may be one or more slender filaments called *barbels,* functioning as organs of touch, taste, or smell. A broad plate-like structure supported mainly by one bone, the *operculum,* covers the gills. Extending along the lower margin of the *operculum* is a membrane, which is supported by bony splints called *branchiostegals.* Between the operculum and the eyes is the region called the cheek. Under the operculum are the *gills,* consisting of a bony arch bearing tooth-like *gill rakers* on the front and reddish (when fresh) *gill filaments* behind. The gill rakers vary in shape from short and stubby to long and slender.

The body can be divided into the *trunk* and *caudal peduncle (see* pl. 2). The caudal peduncle is the narrow wrist-like part in front of the tail fin. The lower part of the trunk surrounding the intestines is the *abdomen.* There are several types of fins, not all of which are found on every fish. The unpaired fins are as follows: on the back is (are) the *dorsal fin(s);* on the upper caudal peduncle, the fleshy tab-like *adipose fin;* on the rear end of the body, the *caudal fin;* and on the underside just in front of the caudal peduncle, the *anal fin(s).* The following paired fins may be present: the *pectoral fins* immediately behind the gill cover and the *pelvic fins* behind or below the pectorals. Above the pelvic fin is sometimes found a triangular *fleshy appendage* for streamlining the fin when it is not extended. The fins, except for the adipose, are supported by slender rods called *rays.* These may be either *soft rays* (jointed and usually flexible), or spiny rays often simply called *spines* (unjointed and usually stiff and pointed). Both the large and small soft rays in the fin are included when counts are mentioned in the text (for the sake of consistency).

The body is usually covered with *scales,* which provide a flexible protective cover for the fish. When the scales are rounded and smooth, as in trout, they are called *cycloid (see* pl. 4). When the scales bear small points on the hind edge making them rough to the touch as in perch, they are called *ctenoid.* The scales take the form of knob-like *scutes* in the sturgeons. Some fishes, such as the eel and even at times the trout, may appear to have no scales. Here, scales are present but are so minute or so deeply imbedded as to be inconspicuous. Of the fishes in this guide, only the catfishes are actually without scales. Scales have growth rings much as do trees. The rings may bunch closely during the slow growth of winter. The areas of bunched rings may be designated as *annual rings.* By counting the annual rings one may determine the fish's age. The scale edge may be absorbed during spawning, producing a *spawning check.* Rapid growth in the sea-years of sea-running fish may produce more widely spaced rings. Thus an expert may learn much of a fish's history by "reading" its scales.

A thin layer of skin covers the fish, including the scales. In the skin are the *mucous cells* which make a slippery fluid, and the colour cells or *chromatophores* which give the fish its colour. The colour varies with maturity and habitat. Colour differences may occur between young and adult, immature and ripe fish, fishes on a dark mud and on light sand bottom.

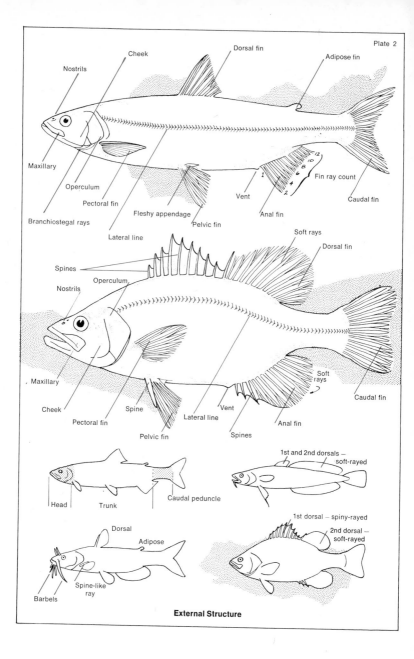

Plate 2

Nostrils · Cheek · Dorsal fin · Adipose fin

Maxillary · Operculum · Pectoral fin · Branchiostegal rays · Fleshy appendage · Pelvic fin · Lateral line · Vent · Anal fin · Fin ray count · Caudal fin

Soft rays · Spines · Dorsal fin · Operculum · Nostrils

Maxillary · Cheek · Pectoral fin · Spine · Pelvic fin · Lateral line · Vent · Spines · Soft rays · Anal fin · Caudal fin

Head · Trunk · Caudal peduncle

1st and 2nd dorsals — soft-rayed

Dorsal · Adipose · Spine-like ray · Barbels

1st dorsal — spiny-rayed · 2nd dorsal — soft-rayed

External Structure

6

Along the middle of the side one may notice a line, the *lateral line.* It usually consists of a buried tube extending from head to tail, which opens to the exterior through pores in the scales. In the tube are tiny sense cells. A similar sensory system is found on the head.

Teeth may be borne on the tongue, on the floor of the mouth between the gill arches, on the roof of the mouth, on the *pharyngeal bones* behind the gills, as well as on the jaws. Minnows have teeth only on the pharyngeal bones. In the freshwater drum the pharyngeal teeth are flat, heavy and pebble-like; they are used for crushing shell-fish.

Water flows in the mouth, through the gill slits, and over the gill filaments which extract oxygen and pass off carbon dioxide. The water then exits from under the operculum. The mouth cavity narrows to the *esophagus* and is usually followed by a j-shaped stomach (*see* pl. 3). The narrow pyloric region following the stomach may bear little finger-like pouches called *pyloric caeca.* The intestine continues to the *anus.* The anus and the exit for the urine and the eggs or sperm is called the *vent.* The *heart* lies in its own small cavity behind and below the gills. The *liver,* usually large and red or orange-coloured, lies in the front part of the body cavity. Associated with it is the small green *gall bladder.* In the upper cavity is the usually thin-walled, pink, balloon-like organ, the *gas bladder* (also called swim bladder). It helps buoy up the fish and may also be used in breathing, hearing or sound-making. The long dark organs that run along the underside of the backbone are the *kidneys.* Below them lie the egg-producing *ovaries* or sperm-producing *testes.* A small *urinary bladder* lies in the hind end of the body cavity.

The skeleton of a fish (*see* pl. 4) includes the skull, the vertebral column with its one to three sets of ribs, and the supports for the fins. The skull includes the *cranium,* housing the brain, and the jaws, gill arches and covers. Behind the skull is the bow-like shoulder girdle that supports the pectoral fin. The pelvic fins are supported by a small pelvic girdle. In the inner-ear portion of the skull are *otoliths,* small bones loose in a fluid-filled chamber. These assist the fish in sensing changes in direction. The large ones in the freshwater drum are sometimes called "lucky stones".

Biology

Locomotion

Fishes propel themselves mainly by flexing their bodies. Fishes deprived of their fins can swim nearly as rapidly as those retaining their fins. At least in some fishes, each of the fins may be employed to some extent for propulsion, particularly at lower speeds. But usually they have more specialized functions. The dorsal and anal fins assist in holding the body upright, and in preventing sway. The paired fins are used in braking, in turning, or sometimes as props. The caudal fin is used as a rudder and to some extent in propulsion.

Migration and Reproduction

Many fishes make extensive directed journeys or migrations at some life stage. These may be for the sake of feeding or reproduction. Fishes often seek specialized conditions in which to lay their eggs. Generally, clear, well-oxygenated waters are sought. Many fishes, such as the Atlantic and Pacific salmons and the rainbow smelt, run

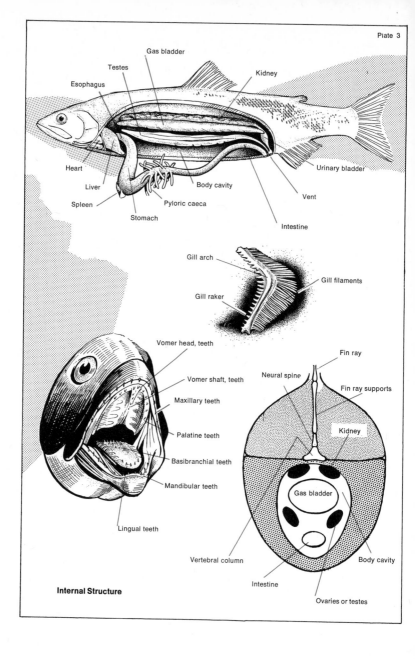

Plate 3

Gas bladder

Testes

Esophagus

Kidney

Heart

Liver

Body cavity

Spleen

Pyloric caeca

Stomach

Urinary bladder

Vent

Intestine

Gill arch

Gill filaments

Gill raker

Vomer head, teeth

Fin ray

Neural spine

Vomer shaft, teeth

Fin ray supports

Maxillary teeth

Palatine teeth

Kidney

Basibranchial teeth

Mandibular teeth

Gas bladder

Lingual teeth

Vertebral column

Body cavity

Intestine

Ovaries or testes

Internal Structure

from the sea into freshwater streams to lay their eggs. These are called *anadromous* fishes. Those that run from fresh water to the sea to lay their eggs, like the American eel, are called *catadromous* fishes.

Most fishes lay their eggs freely in the water, there to be fertilized by the male. The eggs may float in the water as in the goldeye, be shed between the stones on a rocky bottom as in the lake charr, be laid in an open nest as in the sunfishes, or be buried in a redd as in the case of the salmons. In other cases the eggs may be internally fertilized and the young born alive. Generally the less care given the eggs and young, the greater the quantity of eggs that are laid. Thus the burbot, which may lay up to a million eggs, gives them no care, whereas the smallmouth bass lays up to about ten thousand in a nest and guards the eggs and young.

Senses

The usual sense organs of sight, smell, taste, touch, balance and hearing are found in fishes, in addition to the lateral line.

Fishes are generally somewhat short-sighted, perhaps in response to the conditions of low visibility in water. Their eyes are usually quite sensitive and can detect objects at lower light intensities than ours can. Many fishes can distinguish colours.

Smell can be well developed in fishes. In fact once salmon are back in fresh water, they relocate their home stream in which to spawn by using their sense of smell. Organs of taste may be located in the mouth, or as in the case of catfishes, on the barbels and on the body.

Hearing is developed in fishes but not nearly as well as in man. Sounds with higher frequency are not heard. But the sensitivity of hearing in some fishes is increased by contact of the gas bladder with the inner ear. In the herrings and the mooneyes the contact is direct, while in the minnows and catfishes a chain of bones conducts the sound from the gas bladder to the ear.

The lateral line is found only in fishes and a few aquatic amphibians. It detects currents, waves and low frequency sounds that help the fish to navigate, locate prey, and avoid predators. It becomes particularly useful under conditions of low visibility.

Feeding

Fishes usually begin their life feeding on minute animal and plant life, called plankton. Because this is almost universal it is not mentioned in the text under feeding habits. Some, like kokanee and cisco, continue feeding on plankton throughout their lives. Others, such as the walleye and lake charr, may specialize on fish, or like the freshwater drum on molluscs, or like the carp on a variety of plant and animal foods. Gradually, through evolution, the structure of a fish may become adapted to the type of food eaten. Those preying on fish usually have large jaws well provided with sharp teeth; plankton feeders have poorly developed teeth and are equipped with numerous long gill rakers to strain out plankton; mollusc feeders like the freshwater drum may have huge pebble-like teeth with which to crush the shells.

Growth and Age

Fish, unlike mammals and birds, continue to grow throughout their lives. They do not stop growing when they have reached a certain

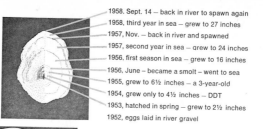

1958. Sept. 14 — back in river to spawn again

1958, third year in sea — grew to 27 inches

1957, Nov. — back in river and spawned

1957, second year in sea — grew to 24 inches

1956, first season in sea — grew to 16 inches

1956, June — became a smolt — went to sea

1955, grew to 6½ inches — a 3-year-old

1954, grew only to 4½ inches — DDT

1953, hatched in spring — grew to 2½ inches

1952, eggs laid in river gravel

Plate 4

Summer   Winter

Ridges in the bony layer are widely spaced during fast growth but closely spaced during slow growth. Circular patterns thus formed show age and growth.

Ridged bony layer   Layer of tissue

A scale sliced through

Scales grow with the fish; ridged bony layer spreads over new layers of tissue as they are added to the undersurface of scale.

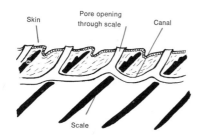

Skin   Pore opening through scale   Canal

Scale

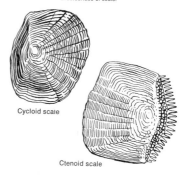

Cycloid scale

Ctenoid scale

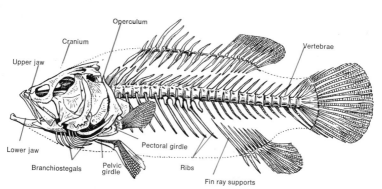

Operculum

Cranium

Upper jaw

Lower jaw

Branchiostegals

Pelvic girdle

Pectoral girdle

Ribs

Fin ray supports

Vertebrae

Scales and Skeleton

size. Growth rate differs from species to species and varies in different waters depending on temperature, food and length of growing season. Growth tapers off after a certain point in each species, resulting in the characteristic maximum size of different species. Thus pumpkinseeds of over a foot in length are unknown whereas lake charr of over 4 feet have been netted. The age attained, like growth, varies from species to species. Few smelt are older than six years while walleye may exceed 10, lake charr 40 years, and lake sturgeon 150 years. See table 1 which presents the average lengths attained at different ages in one particular body of water. Age may be determined from scales, fin rays, otoliths, or other bones. Pl. 4 shows annual rings in the scale of an Atlantic salmon.

Table 1   Age–length relationship of some Canadian sport fishes*

Age in years	1	2	3	4	5	6	7	8	9	10	15	35	50
Fork length (in.)													
Lake sturgeon	10	12	14	16	18	20	22	24	25	26	32	49	62
Lake charr (lake trout)	5	10	14	16	19	21	24	26	28	29	35		
Brook charr (brook trout)	2	5	8	11	14								
Arctic charr	3	6	7	8	10	15	17	18	19				
Dolly Varden		5	8	11	12	13	15	17	17	18			
Brown trout	5	7	9	11	14								
Atlantic salmon	2	4	16	30	38	42	45						
Rainbow trout	4	6	15	21	25	27	29						
Cutthroat trout		8	10	12	13	14							
Chinook salmon	9	18	26	30									
Lake whitefish	5	8	9	11	12	13	14	14	15	16			
Muskellunge	12	20	26	28	30	32	34	36	38	41	54		
Northern pike	6	11	16	20	23	25	28	31	33	34	40		
Striped bass	2	4	9	14	16	18	19						
Smallmouth bass	2	5	7	9	11	12	13	14	15	16			
Largemouth bass	3	6	9	12	14	16	17	18					
Walleye	4	7	11	12	14	15	17	18	20				
Yellow perch	2	4	5	6	7	8	9						

*Length is average fork length at that age from a single location. This is a crude indication only, as growth varies from place to place.

How to Identify Fishes

First look closely at the fish, note its general shape and colour, spread the fins and observe their form and placement, determine whether the jaws are toothed and whether when closed the upper jaw reaches or passes the eye. Feel the scales to find if they are ctenoid or cycloid. One can even smell the fish (smelts have a cucumber-like smell). When you have a firm impression of the fish in your mind, go to the *family keys* on the back endpapers. First decide to which of the three major groups it belongs, then within that group decide to which family your fish belongs and turn to the indicated page. Skip these procedures if you know the family. In the two largest and most diverse families, the salmon family and the sunfish family, there is a key to the genera or major groups of species within the family. Determine the genus.

Examine the figures in the species accounts that resemble your fish. Note the important identifying features indicated by the green diagonal lines and described under "Differ". Find the species that most closely matches all the features of your fish. Check the map to see if the species occurs in the area. Where the choice is between two very similar species the maps may help in identification if the species have different ranges. Lastly, compare your fish with one of the colour photographs (when there is one) in the back of the guide.

It is important to remember that certain features of fishes vary. Lake charr may be large-headed in one lake and small-headed in the next. A rainbow trout caught over a light sandy bottom is often much lighter in colour than one caught over a mud bottom. There are other characters that are more constant in a species and which show differences between species. These are the characters described under "Differ" and indicated in the figures. But even these characters occasionally vary, and to be certain of identification it is best to use all the characters mentioned.

Under some circumstances one may wish the identification of an expert. In the case of record-sized fish, difficult to identify specimens, or specimens found outside the known range of the species, provincial or federal fisheries departments or museums are often helpful. *See* the following directions for preserving specimens. The authors would be pleased to hear from readers in this regard or in regard to any comments on the book.

Preserving Fishes for Identification

To preserve rarities or specimens for identification one may use several methods. The one usually used by scientists is to drop the specimen in 10 per cent formalin — one part of concentrated formalin (obtainable at most drugstores) mixed with 9 parts of water. A slit should be cut into the body cavity of specimens longer than 6 inches to permit penetration of the preservative. The whole fish with intestine and gills should be preserved as these often possess important features.

Alternately, one may freeze the specimen or preserve it in salt. Information on exactly where the fish was caught — body of water, province, distance from nearest town — with date and collector's name should accompany the specimen. Care should be taken in shipping or mailing the specimen to assure that it arrives in good condition. Detailed instructions on preserving may be found in *Methods of Collecting and Preserving Vertebrate Animals,* cited on p. 74.

Specimens may be sent for identification to:

Curator of Fishes,
National Museum of Natural
   Sciences,
National Museums of Canada,
Ottawa, Ontario
K1A 0M8

Department of Ichthyology &
   Herpetology,
Royal Ontario Museum,
100 Queen's Park,
Toronto, Ontario
M5S 2C6

The Angler and His Environment

The sound of a white-throated sparrow calling as the sun lifts the morning mists from the limpid waters of the lake, the dimpling of the surface by an unseen fish, the bite of fresh air in the lungs, a craggy pine standing high — these are part of the unspoiled peace and beauty and loneliness of nature that we wish to save and enjoy. To visit these things is to be restored; even to know they exist gives satisfaction. Some pretend that their value can be measured in dollars or gross national product. But what price can be placed on the haunting call of a loon floating unseen in the night?

The air, water and land in which life occurs form a bubble around the planet Earth, called the biosphere. This biosphere is a continuum or unit because of the movement and interchange of energy and matter among its various primary elements. Winds, for example, transport fine particles or gases around the globe at 30° North Latitude in about two weeks. Overgrazing on land may cause erosion and silting of spawning beds; carbon dioxide from internal combustion engines disperses into the atmosphere and eventually into the oceans and living systems; chemicals sprayed on forests may pass into stream water and end in the sea.

Matter and energy added to the environment may transform or dissipate or they may not, but they do not disappear. DDT may change to DDE, carbon monoxide to carbon dioxide, and sulphur dioxide to sulphuric acid. In some cases, like DDT in a chain of foods, the pollutant may be concentrated. Mercury used on the continents has turned up in ocean swordfish. Continued input into the environment over a sufficient period of time will eventually result in an output. As the Honourable Jack Davis, Minister of the Environment, has recently said, "No lake however large and no sky however vast is capable of absorbing man's effluents forever."

In some ways the slow deterioration of the environment is worse than a fast deterioration, for changes over the decades may be unnoticed and unrectified. But our power to change is now augmented.

Until the last century the smaller number of men and their limited use of energy meant a low capacity to influence the environment. The world population is now doubling about every 35 years. The level of pollution per capita can be reduced, but whatever level is established per capita, the total pollution will be related to the number of people. In Canada our population has doubled since 1940. Our electric power generation per capita — one index of our capacity to make changes — has quadrupled since 1940. This alliance of number and power poses a sombre reality.

Human influence on the aquatic environment may be summarized under four headings — chemical, thermal, physical, and biological pollution. Some changes may result in more than one type of pollution.

Chemical pollutants include industrial, agricultural and human wastes, and chemicals such as solvents, pesticides, and fertilizers. These may adversely influence the food, growth, behaviour, respiration or reproduction of fishes, kill them outright or make them unsafe to eat. Some chemicals extract oxygen from the water directly, others indirectly, by encouraging the growth of algae. *Synergistic toxicity* may result when two or more pollutants interact, resulting in a toxic effect greater than the added individual effects.

Thermal pollution is the addition of heat energy to the atmosphere or water. Raised temperature may result from the use of fresh or saline waters for cooling in thermal power plants, or by passage of water through the hydroelectric turbines of dams. The impoundment of river water by dams may change the temperature regime downstream by tapping the warmer surface water or the cooler deoxygenated bottom water. The reduced flow of water in summer is subject to over-heating. The ecology of the water behind the dam is changed from river-like to lake-like. This may modify the fish fauna.

Some of man's activities have purely physical effects. Dams may act as barriers to fish migration. Industrial, irrigational, or municipal intakes may sharply reduce or interrupt river flow. Suspended matter in the water may interfere with normal functioning of the gills, suffocate eggs, and reduce the penetration of light into the water. Silting, resulting from placer mining, erosion of farmland, or deforestation, and collections of cans, bottles, sawdust, bark, or waste fibre may cover the bottom, burying feeding or spawning areas. Dredging, gouging from log drives, or boat traffic may, on the other hand, excavate and destroy the same habitats.

Biological pollution may result from the introduction, elimination, or change in numbers of a particular species of animal or plant. The animal species involved may be predators, competitors, prey or parasites. Changes in the status of a plant species may modify the shelter, space, food supply, or oxygen that they provide. This applies to terrestrial as well as to aquatic plants since terrestrial plants influence such factors as erosion, temperature, and runoff. As we are beginning to learn, a change in status of an animal or plant species may have multiple ramifications. The introduction of a new sport fish may have a whole chain of consequences unrelated to the intent of the introduction, as was learned when carp were transplanted to North America. On the whole, it is probably better not to introduce new species especially if in-depth ecological studies have not been made.

The loss of a species is a tragedy to be avoided. A species once lost is forever gone. The Canadian populations of 17 species or subspecies are provisionally considered rare or endangered (McAllister 1970a). The paddlefish has not been recorded from Canadian waters for over 50 years. The blue walleye of Lake Erie is now probably extinct.

Is it worth trying to save or restore the environment? Can it be done? What can I do? To the first question, what finer heritage can we leave to future generations than fauna and flora, land, air and water in untrammelled state. To the second, the environment can be restored: salmon are again ascending the once heavily polluted Thames River in England. Closer to home, at Saint-Donat, Quebec, it was announced in the summer of 1972 that the water of Lake Archambault had been purified and had become almost suitable for drinking. And there will probably be no easier time than now to set aside land for future parks. The creation of aquatic parks should also be considered (McAllister 1970b). The following paragraphs suggest answers to the third question.

As a citizen or as a member of an anglers' association, conservation group (Mosquin and Myers 1970), or park society you can write letters or submit briefs to municipal, provincial and federal governments and to industries. Ask for stronger anti-pollution laws — and enforcement; request land zoning so that urban sprawl does not eat up wilderness and agricultural land; support construction and costs of sewage treatment plants. Press for the production of silent, efficient, and exhaust-free motors.

As an individual you can educate your children and practise what you profess. Install septic tanks at the cottage, collect and dispose of litter (your own and that of others) at dumps, avoid paving the bottoms of our lakes and rivers with plastic bottles and cans, stop using pesticides, buy silent outboard motors and keep them tuned or, better still, when fishing use a canoe or rowboat. Plant trees for the future.

With his present numbers and power man must change his philosophy towards the environment. Recycling must replace disposal. The quick solution, the fast buck, the local benefit, and the growth ethic must be relegated to the past along with other archaic viewpoints. In their place must be considered the long-term benefit to all mankind. From the Indian and the Innuit we must learn to live in harmony with nature.

References

(A list of conservation organizations in Canada may be obtained for $1.00 from W. J. Cody, Business Manager, *Canadian Field-Naturalist,* Plant Research Institute, Central Experimental Farm, Ottawa.)

La Banque Royale du Canada. 1959. *La préservation des ressources du Canada, son sol, ses forêts et ses cours d'eau.* Montreal, 44 pp.

Canada, Resources for Tomorrow Conference, Montreal, 1961. *Background papers.* 2 vols. Supplementary volume, 1962. Ottawa, Queen's Printer. 2 vols, $10.00; supplementary vol. $1.00.

Conservation Council of Ontario. 1956. *A report on fish and wildlife conservation.* Toronto, 64 pp.

Dymond, J. R., ed. 1964. *Fish and wildlife, a memorial to W. J. K. Harkness.* Toronto, Longmans, 214 pp., illus.

Efford, Ian A., and Barbara M. Smith. 1972. *Energy and the environment.* H. R. MacMillan Lectures for 1971. Vancouver, B.C., Institute of Resource Ecology, University of British Columbia. 220 pp., $2.00.

Haig-Brown, Roderick L. 1961. *The living land.* British Columbia Natural Resources Conference. Toronto, Macmillan, 269 pp., illus.

Laval, Université. 1953. *Conservation des richesses naturelles renouvelables.* Joint Symposium of Le Comité et l'Association canadienne-française pour l'Avancement des Sciences. Quebec, Les Presses universitaires, 202 pp.

Maheux, Georges S. 1953. *Conservation des richesses naturelles renouvelables.* Quebec, Les Presses de l'Université Laval, 203 pp., soft cover. $4.00.

McAllister, D. E. 1970a. *Rare or endangered Canadian fishes.* Canadian Field-Naturalist 84 (1): 5-8.

McAllister, D. E. 1970b. *Proposal for aquatic parks and reserves in Canada.* Canadian Field-Naturalist 84 (2): 97.

Miller, Richard B. 1962. *A cool curving world.* Toronto, Longmans, 202 pp., illus.

Mosquin, Theodore, and M. T. Myres. 1970. *Directory of natural history, conservation and environment organizations in Canada/Annuaire des groupes s'occupant d'histoire naturelle, de conservation ou du milieu vivant au Canada.*

Newell, Reginald E. 1971. *The global circulation of atmospheric pollutants.* Scientific American 224 (1): 32-42, illus.

Canadian Nature Federation

Nature Canada, semi-annual periodical (46 Elgin Street, Ottawa, Ontario K1P 5K6), annual subscription: $6.00.

Canadian Wildlife Federation

Wildlife News, bilingual periodical published in Ottawa (149 Carling Street), annual subscription: $5.00.

National and Provincial Parks Association of Canada

Park News, periodical published in Toronto (43 Victoria Street, Room 18, Toronto 1), annual subscription: $5.00.

THE ANGLER'S PERSONAL CATCH RECORD

(A record of the species caught; tick those species you have captured.)

lake sturgeon_____

American shad_____

goldeye_____

mooneye_____

lake charr (lake trout)_____

brook charr (brook trout)_____

Arctic charr_____

Dolly Varden_____

brown trout_____

Atlantic salmon_____

rainbow or steelhead trout_____

cutthroat trout_____

chinook salmon_____

coho salmon_____

sockeye salmon or kokanee_____

chum salmon_____

pink salmon_____

Arctic grayling_____

inconnu_____

mountain whitefish_____

lake whitefish_____

cisco_____

rainbow smelt_____

muskellunge_____

northern pike_____

chain pickerel_____

carp_____

tench_____

fallfish_____

creek chub_____

northern squawfish_____

yellow bullhead_____

channel catfish_____

brown bullhead_____

burbot_____

Atlantic tomcod_____

white bass_____

white perch_____

striped bass_____

bluegill_____

pumpkinseed_____

longear sunfish_____

green sunfish_____

redbreast sunfish_____

smallmouth bass_____

largemouth bass_____

black crappie_____

white crappie_____

rock bass_____

walleye_____

sauger_____

yellow perch_____

freshwater drum_____

FAMILY AND SPECIES ACCOUNTS

Sturgeon family
Famille des esturgeons
Acipenseridae

The long snout with barbels and mouth on the underside, the rows of scutes along the sides and top of the body (*see* below, a scute from the side), and the heterocercal tail with its long upper lobe enable quick recognition of the sturgeons. The sturgeons, one of the more primitive kinds of bony fishes, are found in fresh waters of the northern hemisphere. Some run to the sea.

Five species are found in Canada. The white sturgeon, *Acipenser transmontanus* Richardson, occasionally caught on bait in B.C., reaches tremendous sizes. Specimens of up to 20 feet and 1,800 pounds have been reported in the Fraser R. Because of the length of time needed to reach maturity — about two decades in the lake sturgeons — careful management is needed to maintain sturgeon populations.

Scute

Lake sturgeon
Esturgeon de lac
Acipenser fulvescens **Rafinesque**

Differ: from other fishes in having barbels in front of mouth under a long snout, rows of bony plates on body, and the upper lobe of caudal fin long.

Size: to 7½ ft. and 310 lb. — one commercially caught in Batchawana Bay, L. Superior, Ont. One of 35 lb. 8 oz. was angled from the Winnipeg R., Man., by Edmund Richscheid, June 1966.

Notes: live in larger rivers and lakes usually in depths less than 30 ft. Consume insect larvae, molluscs, and crayfish from the bottom with their protrusible mouth. Spawn in spring in rapid water in rivers or wave-washed lake shores. Attain great ages; a 208-pounder from Lake of the Woods was 152 years

old. Do not mature until about 20 years of age. Baited hook and line are used in angling. For further details read *The Lake Sturgeon* by W. J. K. Harkness and J. R. Dymond, Ontario Department of Lands and Forests, 1961, 121 pp.; or *Sturgeons*, by V. D. Vladykov, Album 5, "Fishes of Quebec", Quebec Department of Tourism, Fish and Game, 1955, 12 pp.

Herring family
Famille des harengs
Clupeidae

Members of the herring family usually have a row of sharp-edged scales along the belly. Unlike most fishes, they have no lateral-line canal along the side. Herrings are found in seas around the world, with some species venturing into or remaining in fresh water. Nine species are known from Canada.

The flesh of herrings is delicious, but bony. In fact, in the Maritimes it is said that after a meal of gasparot (a close relative of the shad), it's hard to get your shirt off! Only one species, the American shad, is regularly angled for in Canada. There is a minor sport fishery for the shad in the Maritimes and in Quebec.

Silver doctor

American shad
Alose savoureuse
Alosa sapidissima (Wilson)

Differ: from other fishes in the presence of a dark spot on the shoulder and usually with fainter spots behind, a saw-like row of scales on the belly, and in the two flap-like scales on the caudal fin.

Size: to 30 in. and 14 lb., rarely more than 9 lb. The angling record is one of 7 lb. 2 oz. (Massachusetts).

Notes: the young descend to the sea in the fall of their first year. Feed on plankton and small fishes. As early as their fourth year, in late spring or early summer, they cease to feed, and ascend rivers to spawn. Between 25,000 to 156,000 eggs may be spawned per female. Eggs settle on the bottom and are given no care. Will take wet flies, small silver spoons or a small minnow. One must reel in the lure carefully because the mouth is delicate. Native to the Atlantic coast, it has been introduced to the Pacific coast. Read *The American Shad and the Alewife,* by J. M. Roy, Album 8, "Fishes of Quebec," Quebec Department of Tourism, Fish and Game, 1969, 24 pp.

Mooneye family
Famille des laquaiches
Hiodontidae

The mooneyes are deep silvery or golden fishes with the dorsal fin behind the middle of the body. Unlike the minnow family they possess teeth in the jaws and unlike the salmon family they lack an adipose fin. The curious fold of skin between the lower jaws, the gular fold, is a vestige left from the bony gular plate possessed by their ancestors. Connections between the gas bladder and the inner ear in these fishes are probably used in hearing and possibly suggest that the mooneyes may produce sounds.

The mooneyes are found only in the fresh waters of North America, where there are two living species. One is well known to gourmets. They are now being recognized as fine sport on light tackle. The line must be drawn in carefully.

Gular fold

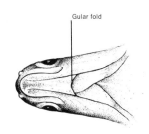

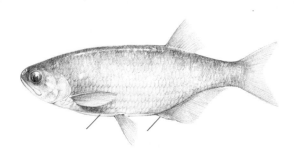

Goldeye
Laquaiche aux yeux d'or
Hiodon alosoides (Rafinesque), col. pl. 4-A
Differ: from other fishes in the toothed jaws, the gular fold across the chin, the far-back dorsal fin, and the almost vertical rows of scales; from the mooneye in having a sharp keel on the belly in front of the pelvics, and in the anal fin beginning in front of the dorsal fin.
Size: to 4 lb. in Alberta, 1967. One of 3 lb. was angled in Manitoba, 1970. Average less than 1 lb.
Notes: dwell in rivers and lakes, often in swift and silty waters below dams and falls. Feed on aquatic and terrestrial insects, snails, crustaceans, and fish. Semi-buoyant eggs are laid in spring. Being surface feeders, they make a spirited response to wet and dry flies or to a grasshopper or worm floated on a short line from a bobber. Forms the

delicacy "Winnipeg goldeye" when smoked. Palatable unsmoked if cleaned and sprinkled with salt overnight before cooking. For further details read *Goldeye in Canada* by W. A. Kennedy and W. M. Sprules, Fisheries Research Board of Canada Bulletin no. 161, 1968, 45 pp.

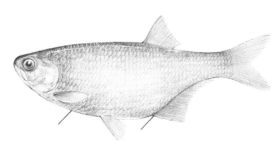

Mooneye
Laquaiche argentée
Hiodon tergisus Lesueur
Differ: from other fishes in the toothed jaws, the gular fold across the chin, the far-back dorsal fin, and the almost vertical rows of scales; from the goldeye in lacking a sharp keel on the belly in front of the pelvics, and in the anal fin beginning under the dorsal fin.
Size: to 17½ in. and 2 lb. 7 oz. (Ohio). One of 2 lb. 2 oz. was angled from Lac du Bonnet, Man., by W. J. Sherk, 1965.
Notes: live in clear rivers, streams and in shallow waters of lakes. Feed on fishes, insects, molluscs and plankton.

Spawn in spring in rivers and streams. females laying 10 to 20 thousand eggs. Will take flies and spinning lures.

Salmon family
Famille des saumons
Salmonidae

The salmon family is marked, like the smelt and catfish families, by having a small fleshy adipose fin. The salmons are easily distinguished from the catfishes, which have barbels. Unlike the smelts, the salmons have a deeper body, a fleshy appendage above the pelvic fins, and pelvic fins starting behind the front of the dorsal fin. Native to the northern hemisphere, the salmonids live wholly in fresh water or spend part of their lives in the sea.

Over 30 species of salmonids are found in Canada, including the Pacific salmons, the Atlantic salmon and trouts, the charrs, the whitefishes, ciscoes, round whitefishes and the grayling. One of the most important families of sport fishes; 18 are of interest to the angler. They are all lovers of cool water. Several spawn in streams, excavating a depression in gravel called a redd; there the eggs are laid, fertilized, and buried. The following life-history stages may be found — *alevin:* just-hatched young still with yolk sac; *parr:* young with dark ovoid blotches along the side; *smolt:* young with silver sides, ready to migrate downstream; *kelt:* spawned-out adult. Often the adults "home" to lay their eggs in the stream where they themselves were hatched.

For an account of the Pacific salmons, see *Canada's Pacific Salmon,* by Roderick L. Haig-Brown, rev. ed., Ottawa, Department of Fisheries and Forestry, 1967, 23 pp.

Plate 5

Salmon subfamily
Salmoninae
• Fine scales — 19 or more from dorsal to lateral line
• Teeth moderate — conical
• Dorsal small and behind pectoral

Scale count

#1

#7

Whitefish subfamily
Coregoninae
• Big scales — 13 or fewer from dorsal to lateral line
• Teeth minute and velvet-like
• Dorsal small and behind pectoral

Head
Shaft
Vomerine teeth

Nostril

Charrs — *Salvelinus*, see pp. 26 – 27
• Light-spotted back, spots light grey to red
• Teeth only on head of vomer
• Only 8 – 12 anal rays (all counted)
• May survive spawning

Inconnu — *Stenodus*, see p. 33
• Upper jaw past mid-eye
• Bands of velvet-like teeth on vomer and palatines
• 1 flap between nostrils
• Snout tip pointed

Shaft
Vomerine teeth

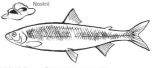

Nostril

True trouts & Atlantic salmon — *Salmo*, see pp. 28 – 29
• Dark-spotted back
• Teeth on shaft of vomer
• Only 9 – 15 anal rays (all counted)
• May survive spawning

Round whitefishes — *Prosopium*, see p. 33
• Upper jaw short of mid-eye
• Teeth weak or lacking
• 2 flaps between nostrils
• Snout tip rounded

Shaft
Vomerine teeth

Nostril

Pacific salmons — *Oncorhynchus*, see pp. 30 – 32
• Dark-spotted back or no spots
• Teeth on shaft of vomer
• 16 or more anal rays (all counted)
• Dies after spawning

Whitefishes — *Coregonus*, see p. 34
• Upper jaw short of mid-eye
• Teeth weak or lacking
• 1 flap between nostrils
• Snout tip rounded or pointed

Grayling subfamily
Thymallinae
• Big scales — 11 or fewer from dorsal to lateral line
• Teeth minute
• Dorsal long, its front above the pectoral

Pictorial Key to Genera of Salmon Family

Lake charr or lake trout
Touladi ou truite de lac
Salvelinus namaycush (Walbaum)

Differ: from other charrs in the light marks on the dark dorsal fin, greyish instead of coloured spots on the side, and in the well-forked caudal fin. Lower fins unmarked. More pyloric caeca, 90 plus, than any other charr.

Size: to 50 in. and 102 lb. — one netted in L. Athabasca, Sask. The angling record is one of 65 lb. in Great Bear L., N.W.T., August 8, 1970. A 63-pounder was angled in L. Superior in 1952.

Notes: dwell in cool waters of lakes and sometimes rivers, go deep when the surface warms. Feed on fishes, insect larvae, and plankton. In fall, spawn on rocky or gravel reefs. A hybrid between the

lake and brook charrs, known as the wendigo (or splake) has been planted in many lakes (see col. pl. 4-B). "Lakers" may be caught in shallow water by lure, bait or fly casting; in deep water by trolling with a flasher above the lure or bait.

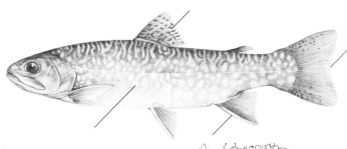

Brook charr or brook trout
Omble de fontaine ou truite mouchetée
Salvelinus fontinalis (Mitchill), col. pl. 4-C

Differ: from other charrs in the dark spots on the dorsal fin, red spots with blue haloes on side, wavy marks on back, and the square or slightly forked tail. Leading edge of lower fins dark with white border. No teeth behind the tongue and between gills (see pl. 3) unlike other charrs.

Size: to 31½ in. and 14½ lb., the world record, angled by Dr. W. J. Cook, Nipigon R., Ont., July 1916.

Notes: live in cool clear fresh waters, may run to the sea. Spawn Oct. to Dec. on riffles or beaches. Feed on insects,

fish, crayfish, molluscs. These elegant fish respond to fly, spin, and worm fishing. The "aurora trout," a subspecies known in Gamble Twp. and Timiskaming and Cochrane Districts, Ont., differs in lacking wavy marks on the back and in having only 1-4 red spots below the lateral line.

Arctic charr
Omble chevalier

Salvelinus alpinus (Linnaeus), col. pl. 5-A
Differ: from most other charrs in the slightly forked caudal fin, the yellow to red spots on sides, and the fins without dark spots. Best told from the similar Dolly Varden by the range, *see* maps. Sea-run fish are green-backed and silver-sided.
Size: to 34½ in. and 33 lb. (USSR). Angling record is 29 lb. 11 oz., N.W.T., 1968. A 32½-incher was netted in Sylvia Grinnell R., N.W.T. Usually 5-10 lb.
Notes: live in cold streams, rivers and lakes, many migrate to sea. Feed on fish and plankton. Spawn in lakes or rivers in autumn. Most taken on red-devil lures,

spoons or flies. A sport fishery is now developing in the North for this handsome fish. The "Quebec red trout," found in cool southerly Quebec lakes, may represent a distinct form of Arctic charr.

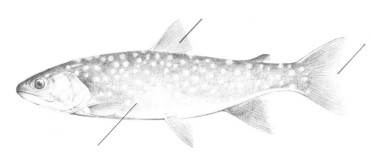

Dolly Varden
Dolly Varden

Salvelinus malma (Walbaum), col. pl. 5-B
Differ: from most other charrs in the slightly forked caudal fin, yellow or red spots on sides, and fins without dark markings. Best told from its close relative the Arctic charr by range, *see* maps. Sea-run fish are green-backed and silver-sided.
Size: to 40½ in. and 32 lb., the angling record (Idaho). A 29-pounder was caught in Kootenay L., B.C. Usually 3-4 lb.
Notes: live in streams and lakes, some run to sea. Feed on fishes, insect larvae, and molluscs. Spawn in streams during

fall. Angled for with artificial lures, flies, spoons, and bait. Although inclined to be logy on the line, in cool swift streams dollies are game.

27

Brown trout
Truite brune
Salmo trutta Linnaeus

Differ: from all other trout and Atlantic salmon *(Salmo)* in having light haloes around some of the dark or coloured spots on the sides. Adipose fin often with red spots, caudal fin not or only weakly spotted. Markings may be poorly developed in silvery sea-run fish. Unlike Atlantic salmon, often have a long upper jaw, red spots on the adipose fin, and a stout caudal peduncle.

Size: to 40 lb. (Tasmania), but angling record is 40½ in. and 39 lb. 8 oz. (Scotland). One of 29 lb. 9 oz. was caught in Wisconsin and one of 28 lb. 8 oz. near St. John's, Nfld., in 1962. Average 1-5 lb.

Notes: live in streams and lakes, some run to sea. Feed on insects, especially surface ones, fish, crayfish and worms. Spawn in streams in fall and early winter. Rise to the dry fly and respond to other lures especially at twilight and after dark. A wary fish, often difficult to catch. Introduced from Europe.

Atlantic salmon
Saumon atlantique
Salmo salar Linnaeus

Differ: sea-run fish differ from other trout *(Salmo)* in the short jaw, the dark x-shaped spots above the lateral line, the slender caudal peduncle, and the caudal fin not or only weakly spotted (but ouananiche are spotted as in the inset). Unlike brown trout, have a short upper jaw, lack red spots on adipose fin, and have a slender caudal peduncle.

Size: to 79 lb., 2 oz., the angling record (Norway). One of 55 lb. was angled in Cascapédia R., Que., and one of 52½ lb. in the Margaree R., N.S. Average 5-10 lb.

Notes: live in lakes and streams. May run to sea, or remain in fresh water their whole life — then called ouananiche. Feed on insects, fishes, and amphipods.

Spawn in streams in fall. Angled for by fly fishing. One of the finest sport fishes in Canada, with its graceful rise, its line-melting runs, and vigorous leaps. Read V. Legendre; and *The Atlantic Salmon*, by Lee Wulff (New York, A.S. Barnes), 1958, 222 pp.

Rainbow trout or steelhead
Truite arc-en-ciel
Salmo gairdnerii Richardson, col. pl. 5-C

Differ: from other trout and Atlantic salmon *(Salmo)* in usually having a reddish band along the side, and a dark-spotted body and caudal fin. Adipose fin and sides without red spots. Sides silvery in sea-run fish.

Size: to 42 lb. 2 oz. (Alaska), usually cited as the angling record, but one 36 in. and 52½ lb. was taken in Jewel L., southern B.C. Rainbows average 1-5 lb., steelheads 5-15 lb.

Notes: may spend life wholly in streams or lakes — then called rainbow trout; or run to the sea — then called steelhead; in the interior of B.C. often called "Kamloops trout." But all of these are the

same species. Feed on insects, fish, freshwater shrimp, molluscs, leeches. Spawn in spring in running fresh water. Angled for with flies, plugs, spoons, spinners, and bait. One of the gamest varieties of Canadian sport fishes, with its head-shaking, lure-throwing jumps.

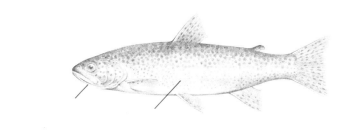

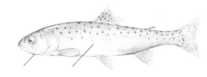

Cutthroat trout
Truite fardée
Salmo clarkii Richardson, col. pl. 6-A

Differ: from all other true trout and Atlantic salmon *(Salmo)* in the two red-streaked grooves between the lower jaws and in having basibranchial teeth behind the tongue and between the gills (*see* pl. 3). There are two subspecies in Canada. The larger coastal subspecies, *Salmo clarkii clarkii* (upper fig.), has many dark spots anteriorly below the lateral line, unlike the interior subspecies, *Salmo clarkii lewisi* (lower fig.). Sides silvery in sea-run fish.

Size: to 39 in. and 41 lb., the angling record (Nevada). Usually ¾-4 lb.

Notes: live in cool lakes and streams. Some coastal populations run to the sea. Feed on fish and insect larvae. Spawn in small streams in spring. A free riser and a staunch fighter, it responds well to flies, spoons, plugs, and bait. An elegant-looking fish.

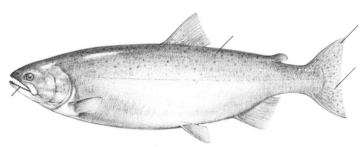

Chinook salmon
Saumon chinook
Oncorhynchus tshawytscha (Walbaum)
Differ: from other Pacific salmon in the moderate-sized spots on the back, dorsal fin, and both lobes of the caudal fin. Have black gums unlike coho. Gill rakers 20-28.
Size: to 126 lb. 3 oz. — a commercially-caught fish (Alaska). The angling record is one of 58½ in. and 92 lb. from the Skeena R., B.C., caught by H. Wichmann, July 1959. Usually 10-50 lb.
Notes: young descend river to sea (or Great Lakes) in their first or second year. After two to seven years on the high seas, they return in the fall to spawn and die in their home river. Adults do not feed in fresh water. Angled for with spoons and

other lures. The musical Indian name, "chinook," now replaces the name. "spring." Chinooks of over 30 lb. are called "tyees." Read *Return to the River: A Story of the Chinook Run*, by Roderick L. Haig-Brown (New York, William Morrow), 1941.

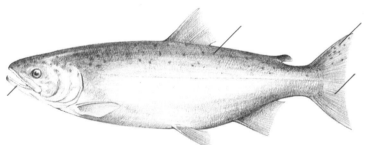

Coho salmon
Saumon coho
Oncorhynchus kisutch (Walbaum)
Differ: from other Pacific salmon in the moderate-sized spots on the back and upper lobe only of the caudal fin. Have white gums unlike chinook. Gill rakers 19-25.
Size: to 33 lb., the angling record (Michigan). One of 31 lb. was caught in Cowichan B., B.C., by Mrs. L. Halberg in 1947. Fish to 38½ in. have been caught. Usually 5-10 lb.
Notes: After reaching from a few weeks to two years of age, the young descend to the sea or to the Great Lakes. They usually return in their third year to spawn in November or December. Adults do not feed in fresh water. Caught by casting

with wet flies like the bucktail, by spinning, trolling with spoons, plugs, jigs, or by bar fishing with bait in the lower course of rivers. The coho is a clean and splendid jumper. Since its introduction in Lake Michigan, it has migrated into the Canadian waters of the lower Great Lakes.

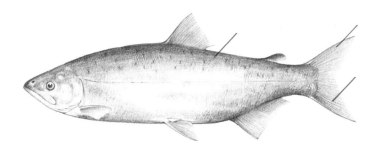

Sockeye salmon or kokanee
Saumon nerka ou kokani
Oncorhynchus nerka (Walbaum)
Differ: from other Pacific salmon in the absence of spots (often fine speckles on back) and the many slender, rough, crowded gill rakers, 30-40. The chum is also unspotted but has only 19-26 gill rakers, these spaced and smooth.
Size: to 33 in. and 15½ lb. in the sea. A kokanee of 26¾ in. and 9 lb. 2 oz. was angled in Echo L., Okanagan district, B.C.; usually about 1 lb.
Notes: the fry develop in a lake, the eggs having been laid in its tributaries or on its shore in fall. After a year or two in the lake they go to sea, returning to spawn in the fall of their fourth or fifth year. But some populations remain in lakes, achieve smaller sizes and are called "kokanee." Kokanee feed on

plankton and insects. Spinners, plugs or flies may be used for kokanee; sockeye may take golf-tee spinners in the lower reaches of rivers. Read *The Sockeye Salmon* by R. E. Foerster, Fisheries Research Board of Canada Bulletin no. 162, 1968, 422 pp.

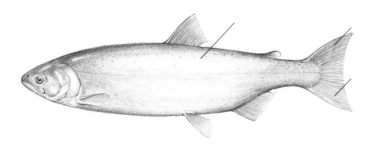

Chum salmon
Saumon keta
Oncorhynchus keta (Walbaum)
Differ: from other Pacific salmon in the absence of spots (may be speckles on back) and the 18-26 short, smooth, spaced gill rakers. The sockeye is also unspotted but has 30 to 40 slender, rough, crowded gill rakers.
Size: to 40 in. and 33 lb. — one taken at Tallheo, Bella Coola, B.C., in July 1951. Usually 8-18 lb.
Notes: shortly after emerging from the redd the fry migrate to sea. In their third to fifth year they return to spawn in fall, usually not far from the sea. But one run

migrates about 2,000 miles up the Yukon River to Teslin L., northern B.C. Do not feed as adults in fresh water but will take dull metal devons.

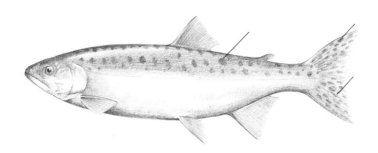

Pink salmon
Saumon rose
Oncorhynchus gorbuscha (Walbaum)

Differ: from other Pacific salmon in the large-sized, often oval spots on the back and both lobes of the caudal fin. Largest spots at least eye-sized. Gill rakers 23-34.

Size: to 30 in. and 10 lb. Usually 3-5 lb.

Notes: like those of the chum, the fry migrate to sea shortly after emerging from the redd. At the age of two, they return home to spawn in coastal streams in fall. Do not feed as adults in fresh water. May be caught on flies, spinners, spoons or with worms. Run strongly but seldom jump when hooked. Introduced into several eastern Canadian waters.

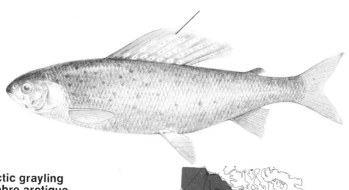

Arctic grayling
Ombre arctique
Thymallus arcticus (Pallas), col. pl. 6-B

Differ: from others of the salmon family in their long mauve-spotted and -edged dorsal fin which begins above the pectoral fin. Have large scales like a whitefish.

Size: to 29⅞ in. and 5 lb. 15 oz. — the world record angled in Katseyedie R., N.W.T., by Jeanne P. Branson. One 5 lb. 7 oz. fish was caught in Great Bear L. and a 5-pounder in Great Slave L., N.W.T. Usually 1-2 lb.

Notes: live in cold clear streams and lakes. Feed largely on insects, aquatic and terrestrial. Spawn in small streams in late spring, burying the eggs in a sand or gravel redd. Rise well to wet and dry flies, particularly the smaller sizes, no. 10 or 12. Freshly caught grayling have the odour of wild thyme. With its burnished purple-grey scales and mauve-edged dorsal the grayling is indeed a noble catch.

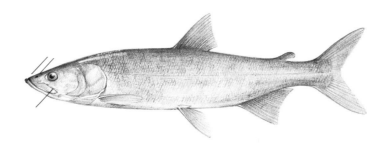

Inconnu
Inconnu
Stenodus leucichthys (Güldenstadt)

Differ: from other whitefishes in the velvet-like bands of teeth on the roof of the mouth, and in the long upper jaw which reaches at least to the rear edge of the pupil. Gill rakers 19-24, short. Body not deep. Nostril with two flaps. Snout profile straight.

Size: to 59¼ in. and 63 lb. in North America — one caught at mouth of the Mackenzie R. in July 1963. In Russia known to 54½ in. and 77 lb. A 75-pounder was reported from Aklavik, N.W.T., in 1956.

Notes: live in large rivers and in shallow waters of lakes. Some populations, as in the lower Mackenzie, run to the sea. Feed mostly on fish. Spawn in flowing water in late summer or early fall. French-Canadian voyageurs, upon discovering this new kind of whitefish, gave it the name *inconnu* or unknown. May be caught trolling or casting with a lure. Eskimos caught them through the ice on barbless hooks or ivory lures.

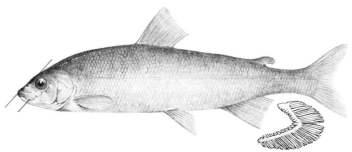

Mountain whitefish
Ménomini des montagnes
Prosopium williamsoni (Girard),
col. pl. 6-C

Differ: from other whitefishes in the short jaws not reaching mid-eye and without noticeable teeth, and in the single nostril flap. Gill rakers 20-26, stubby. Snout profile curved.

Size: to 19 in. and 5 lb. — one angled in the Athabasca R., Alberta, by Orville Welch in June 1963. Usually ½-2 lb.

Notes: live in cool streams and shallow waters of lakes. Feed on aquatic insect larvae and sometimes fish eggs. Spawn in fall in stream riffles without constructing a redd. Will take a sunken fly or hook baited with an insect or maggot. A spirited and popular sport fish in swift mountain streams.

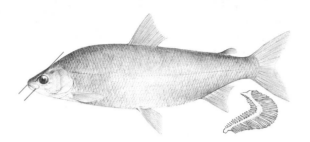

Lake whitefish
Grand corégone
Coregonus clupeaformis (Mitchill),
col. pl. 7-A

Differ: from other whitefishes in the short jaws that fail to reach mid-eye, 23-33 fairly long gill rakers and nostril with two flaps. Snout tip rounded or square, back often humped.

Size: to 28.9 in. and to 26 lb. in the Great Lakes, taken commercially. One of 18 lb. 4 oz. was angled in Lac du Bonnet, Man., by Tony Delormer in 1959. Usually 1-4 lb.

Notes: live in lakes (in deeper water in the south) and rivers. May run to sea in the north. Feed on aquatic insect larvae, molluscs, and plankton. Spawn in late fall or winter on sand, gravel or stones on reefs in lakes or in streams, without making a redd. Often caught by fishing through the ice with bait or lures, casting or trolling with lures, and sometimes by fly casting. By using a rubber band in the line as a shock absorber one can avoid pulling the hook loose from its delicate mouth. Eggs can be made into caviar.

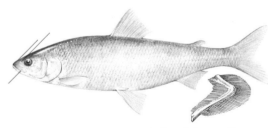

Cisco
Cisco de lac
Coregonus artedii Lesueur, col. pl. 7-B

Differ: from other whitefishes in their short, poorly toothed jaws which do not reach mid-eye, the many long gill rakers, (37-57), and the nostril with two flaps. Snout tip pointed.

Size: up to 21½ in. and to 8 lb. in L. Erie, commercially. Usually about 1 lb.

Notes: live in cold waters of lakes and streams, sometimes migrate to the sea. Feed mainly on plankton but also on aquatic insects and molluscs. Move to deeper waters when the surface warms. Spawn in late fall on gravel or stones in shallow water without making a redd. Can be caught on flies when surface feeding on mayflies. Minnows, insects, larvae, flashy pearl buttons or beads have also been used in open water or in ice fishing. Fished more for its delicate flesh, excellent when smoked, than its gameness.

Smelt family
Famille des éperlans
Osmeridae

The smelt family has 11 species in the waters of the northern hemisphere, but only one is sought for sport in the fresh waters of North America. The smelts resemble small salmonids but lack a triangular fleshy appendage above the pelvic fin. The smelts have the pelvics opposite or before the front of the dorsal fin; in the salmonids the pelvics are behind the front of the dorsal fin. Smelts also have a distinctive cucumber-like odour. They lay their eggs on the bottom where the outer membrane of the egg peels partly off and adheres to the gravel or sand. Anglers most often catch smelts with dipnets during the spawning run on night outings near a bonfire.

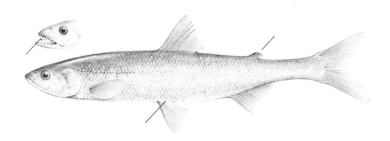

Rainbow smelt
Éperlan arc-en-ciel

Osmerus mordax (Mitchill), col. pl. 7-C
Differ: from the rather similar members of the salmon family in lacking a triangular appendage above the pelvic fin, in having large canine teeth on the roof of the mouth, and in the slender body and small size. There is an adipose fin, and on the tip of the pointed tongue usually a large canine tooth. Have a cucumber-like smell unlike other freshwater sport fishes.
Size: to 15¾ in. total length — one from Sebago L., Maine, caught on hook and line by W. C. Kendall. Weights to 1¼ lb. are reported from L. Champlain and Sebago L. Usually 6-10 in. and 1 lb. 8 oz.
Notes: live in the sea or lakes. Usually in spring near break-up time they ascend streams for spawning, or spawn in lakes.

The eggs adhere to the bottom. Feed on small fishes, crustaceans and worms. They are angled for through the ice, or are netted or scooped out during nightly spawning runs. From a 1912 introduction in L. Michigan the smelts have spread throughout the Great Lakes (native in L. Ontario?).

Pike family
Famille des brochets
Esocidae

Four pikes are known in eastern North America. One of these, the northern pike, ranges northwestward to Alaska and through northern Asia and Europe. A fifth species is found only in eastern Asia. All have a large mouth well armed with teeth, a long narrow body, dorsal and anal fins far back and opposite one another. Voracious fishes of warm waters (except for the northern pike, which reaches far north), they live in streams, ponds, rivers and lakes and are always associated with dense vegetation. They are restricted to fresh water except for the chain pickerel which is sometimes found in brackish water. No care is given to their eggs laid in spring in shallow flooded areas.

There are two main groups, the larger pikes (northern pike and muskellunge) and the smaller pickerels (grass, redfin and chain). Not infrequently they hybridize. The northern pike crosses with the muskellunge to produce the "tiger musky" — like the muskellunge in pattern, but shorter and stockier. The chain pickerel hybridizes readily with the northern pike and the grass and redfin pickerels.

This family, together with the perches and sunfishes, constitutes the most important group of warm-water sport fishes. Many books are written on angling for these fishes.

Branchiostegals

Pores in lower jaws (10)

Muskellunge
Maskinongé

Esox masquinongy Mitchill, col. pl. 8-A

Differ: from other pikes in their potentially great size, silvery colour or pattern of dark spots or bars on light background, cheeks and operculum only half-scaled, 12-18 pores in the underside of the lower jaws and 32-38 branchiostegals.

Size: authentically to 125 lb. and over 6 ft. The angling record is 64½ in. and 69 lb. 15 oz., taken from the St. Lawrence R. (New York). A 51-pounder was angled in Georgian Bay, Ont., in 1963, a 50-pounder in Quebec in 1957. Average 10-15 lb.

Notes: live in lakes and rivers in quiet weedy areas. When spawning pairs move across shallow areas, the fertilized eggs are dropped on vegetation. The eggs hatch in two weeks and the young follow

a food cycle similar to pike. Most often taken trolling with large plugs and feathered spoons or by casting similar baits. One of the largest, most exciting, and sought after of sport fishes. It fights for long periods on the surface and in the air, and even when boated, its thrashing head is dangerous.

Northern pike
Grand brochet

Esox lucius Linnaeus, col. pl. 8-B

Differ: from other pikes in the light oval spotting on dark background, cheek fully and operculum half scaled, 10-11 pores in the lower jaws, and 26-32 branchiostegals. A silver or golden-green mutant without spots called "silver pike" is widespread.

Size: authentically to 53 lb. (Lough Conn, Ireland). Present North American angling record is 52½ in., 46 lb. 2 oz. (New York). One of 45 lb. 15 oz. was taken in Quebec in 1964, and one of 48 in. and 43 lb. in Alberta. Average 4-5 lb.

Notes: live in lakes and rivers in quiet, heavily vegetated areas. At spring break-up a single pair moves into shallow areas and lays batches of eggs on vegetation. Young hatch in two weeks, feed on

plankton until 1-2 in. long, insects and tadpoles until 2-3 in., then fish. Adults consume fish but may take ducklings and frogs, as well as small muskrats. Taken trolling, casting, or still-fishing with large bright lures and bait fish, and ice fishing with bait. Good fighters for short periods, especially in cool water; fight by diving.

37

Chain pickerel
Brochet maillé
Esox niger **Lesueur, col. pl. 8-C**
Differ: from the other adult pikes in their obvious chain-link markings of dark on light, in having only 6-9 pores in the underside of the lower jaws, and scales over whole of the cheek and operculum. Have only 15-16 branchiostegals.
Size: to 31 in. and 9 lb. 6 oz. (Georgia) — is usually cited as the angling record and the biggest specimen known, but one of 10 lb. 4 oz. was angled in Quebec by E. Boulanger in 1956. In Canada they rarely exceed 3-4 lb. and average 1-2 lb.
Notes: live in lakes and sluggish streams among vegetation. Feed largely on fish, crayfish and insects. Spawning is much as in other pikes — in the spring as soon

as ice goes, in swampy, marshy or flooded areas of vegetation. Caught with smaller plugs and spoons, trolling or casting or by still fishing with bait. Some of best catches result from ice fishing with bait. Much like pike in angling quality.

Minnow family
Famille des ménés
Cyprinidae

This is the most varied freshwater fish family in Canada with over 40 species. Only five can be considered of some interest as sport fish. These can be distinguished from the outwardly rather similar members of the salmon and smelt families by the lack of teeth in the jaws and the lack of an adipose fin. Unlike minnows, the mooneye family has teeth in the jaws and a far-back dorsal, the herring family has a keel on the belly, and the more closely related sucker family has flattened sucking lips. The minnows have a chain of bones connecting the gas bladder with the inner ear, which increases the sensitivity of hearing. Minnows are native to all continents except South America, Australia, and Antarctica.

While most minnows are small, some, like the carp and squawfish, attain 2 feet or more. Despite their small size minnows are important as forage and bait fish. However their presence may be detrimental, and minnows should never be dumped in waters in which they do not naturally occur. Although the word minnow is applied to a distinct family of fishes, some people use it improperly to designate any small fish.

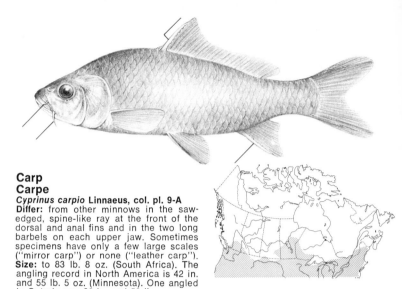

Carp
Carpe

Cyprinus carpio Linnaeus, col. pl. 9-A

Differ: from other minnows in the saw-edged, spine-like ray at the front of the dorsal and anal fins and in the two long barbels on each upper jaw. Sometimes specimens have only a few large scales ("mirror carp") or none ("leather carp").

Size: to 83 lb. 8 oz. (South Africa). The angling record in North America is 42 in. and 55 lb. 5 oz. (Minnesota). One angled in Ontario was 30 in. and 50 lb.

Notes: live in shallow, fairly warm waters of lakes and streams, even when somewhat muddy or polluted. Feed on insect larvae, crustaceans, snails, and plants, often roiling up the bottom. Spawn in vegetated shallows in June and July. A 17-pounder had 2,300,000 eggs. Usually caught still-fishing on doughballs, potatoes, worms, or like baits. Bow-and-arrow fishing is permitted in Ontario. Not a desirable fish in waters with native sport fishes. Introduced from Europe to North America. The influence of anglers from Europe is now increasing the extent to which this often sizable fish is sought. Read *Carp in Canada* by H. R. McCrimmon, Fisheries Research Board of Canada Bulletin no. 165, 1968, 93 pp.

Tench
Tanche

Tinca tinca (Linnaeus)

Differ: from other minnows in having dark fins, deep body, deep caudal peduncle and caudal fin only slightly forked. Reach 25½ in. and 16½ lb. in Europe. Introduced into British Columbia where it is known in Christina, Tugulnuit and Osoyoos Lakes.

Fallfish
Ouitouche
Semotilus corporalis (Mitchill)
Differ: from the creek chub in lacking
the spot on the dorsal fin (which begins
over the pelvic fin base) and in having
dark crescents on the scales. Have a
tiny barbel near corner of mouth. Reach
18 in. and 2 lb. and occur in swift waters
and clear lakes. Like the creek chub,
often provide sport to the younger angler
on fly or bait. Sometimes called "silver
trout" by anglers; are edible.

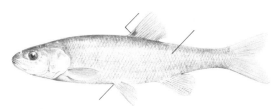

Creek chub
Mulet à cornes
Semotilus atromaculatus (Mitchill)
Differ: from the fallfish in having a dark
spot on the lower front corner of the
dorsal fin (which begins behind the pelvic
fin base) and in lacking the dark crescents on the scales. Have a tiny barbel
near corner of mouth. Reaches 12 in. in
total length.

Northern squawfish
Sauvagesse du Nord
Ptychocheilus oregonensis (Richardson)
col. pl. 9-B
This western species differs from other
minnows in its long, flat, pointed head.
No barbel. It reaches 25 in. and 29 lb.
in Canada. Takes a fly or a small lure.

Catfish family
Famille des barbottes
Ictaluridae

Members of the catfish family can be easily recognized by their adipose fin, long barbels and sharp spines at the front of the dorsal and pectoral fins. Their bodies are smooth and scaleless. This family is indigenous to North America. Other catfish families are known on all the continents except Antarctica; some live in the sea.

Many catfishes rely strongly on their senses of smell, touch, and taste, which enable them to find food in muddy water and at night. Anglers may take advantage of this in selecting baits. The dorsal and pectoral spines of catfishes are sharp. A weak poison emitted by the pectoral spines of some species makes their stings sometimes painful but not dangerous.

Yellow bullhead
Barbotte jaune
Ictalurus natalis **(Lesueur) col. pl. 10-A**
Differ: from the brown bullhead in the white or yellow barbels on the chin and in the 24-27 (usually 25-26) anal rays, and from the channel catfish in the rounded caudal fin. Reach 18.3 in. and 3 lb. 10 oz. (Ohio). Occur in southern Ontario.

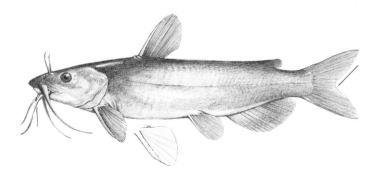

Channel catfish
Barbue de rivière
Ictalurus punctatus (Rafinesque)
Differ: from the bullheads in their deeply forked caudal fin; specimens shorter than 14 in. have dark spots on the sides.
Size: to 62 lb. — the angling record (Louisiana). One of 37 lb. has been reported from Georgian Bay, Ont. Average 2-5 lb.
Notes: live in larger lakes and rivers, often below power dams. Feed on fish, aquatic insects, crayfish, and molluscs. Spawn during spring or summer in rivers. The male guards the eggs and fry. Can be caught on minnows and other

baits which are on the bottom or suspended from a float, or on artificial lures. Night fishing can be productive.

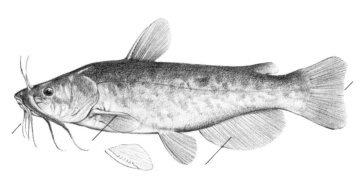

Brown bullhead
Barbotte brune
Ictalurus nebulosus (Lesueur)
Differ: from the yellow bullhead in the grey or black barbels on the chin and in the 21-24 (usually 22-23) anal rays, and from the channel catfish in the very slightly forked or square caudal fin.
Size: to nearly 22 lb. 15 oz. (New Jersey). Usually ¾ to 1½ lb.
Notes: live in warm waters of slow rivers and lakes. Feed on insect larvae, crayfish, worms, molluscs, fish and plant material. Spawn in spring in a saucer-shaped nest. The eggs and young are guarded by the parents. A hook and line

baited with worms, minnows or dough-balls fished on or near the bottom is effective.

43

Cod family
Famille des morues
Gadidae

Members of the cod family are primarily marine, but two species occur in the fresh waters of Canada. Cods can be distinguished from other fishes by the presence of a slender barbel on the midline of the tip of the chin. They usually have either three short dorsal fins, or one short and one long dorsal. The chin barbel and the feeler-like tips of the pelvic fins are used in detecting food.

Prolific fishes, individual burbots may contain over a million eggs, while the smaller tomcod may have over 40,000.

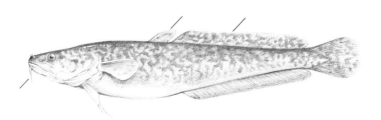

Burbot
Lotte
Lota lota (Linnaeus)

Differ: from other fishes in having a single barbel on the tip of the chin and two dorsal fins (without spines).

Size: to 44 in. or more and to 53 lb. Usually 1-5 lb.

Notes: live in cool waters of rivers and lakes. Feed nocturnally on fish, crayfish, freshwater shrimp and insects. Spawn before break-up in late winter or early spring on sand, gravel or rock bottoms of streams or lakes. The liver, like that of the cod, is a good source of vitamin A. Burbot up to 16 years old have

been caught. Usually caught through the ice on baited hooks fished close to the bottom or, in some areas, by spearing. Has delicately flavoured white flesh.

Atlantic tomcod
Poulamon atlantique
Microgadus tomcod (Walbaum)

Differ: from other fishes in having a single barbel on the tip of the chin and three dorsal fins.

Size: to about 15 in. and 1¼ lb., but seldom more than 8 to 12 in.

Notes: live in the coastal waters of the Atlantic, venturing into estuaries and rivers, and forming permanent freshwater populations in some lakes, such as L. St-Jean, Que. Feed on crustaceans, worms and small fish. Spawn from November to February, often in fresh water, the eggs adhering to the bottom. There is a popular winter sport fishery in Quebec and New Brunswick, jigging

through the ice with hook and line baited with pork liver. Read the account of this species in *Cods,* by V. D. Vladykov, Album 4, "Fishes of Quebec," Quebec Department of Tourism, Fish and Game, 1955, 12 pp.

Temperate bass family
Famille des bars
Percichthyidae

This family is primarily found in warmer waters, but a few species, three in Canada, enter fresh water. They resemble the drum and sunfish families, but differ in having two separate dorsal fins and two spines on the operculum. They differ from the perch family in having three anal spines.

The popular names should not lead the angler to believe that the members of this family are closely related to the black basses or the rock bass in the sunfish family, or to the yellow perch in the perch family. Popular names were often coined without regard to relationships. This is one reason for the use of scientific names.

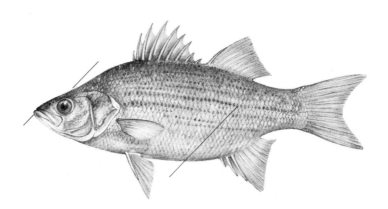

White bass
Bar blanc
Morone chrysops (Rafinesque)

Differ: from the white perch in having the lower jaw projecting and dark stripes on the sides, from the striped bass in having the forehead concave, and the body laterally compressed and deep. Teeth on base of tongue.

Size: to 17 in. and 5 lb. 4 oz. — the angling record and heaviest caught (Kansas). But one of 22.4 in. fork length has been captured. Usually weigh in the neighbourhood of 1 lb.

Notes: live in clear waters of larger lakes and rivers near rock reefs or sand bars. Show some preference for running water, below dams and in stream mouths.

Often school. Feed on small fishes, insects, plankton and crayfish. Spawn in spring over sand, gravel or rock bottoms. Rise to the fly, respond to spinning lures and minnows, both cast and trolled. A scrappy fighter.

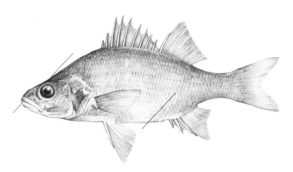

White perch
Bar-perche
Morone americana **(Gmelin), col. pl. 10-B**
Differ: from the white and striped basses in having the tips of the jaws even, and in the absence of stripes from the sides. Also differ from striped bass in having the forehead concave, in the laterally compressed deep body, and the absence of teeth on the base of the tongue.
Size: to 19½ in. and 4 lb. 12 oz. — the angling record and largest caught (Maine). Usually not over 10 in. and ½ lb. inland.
Notes: live along the Atlantic coast mainly in brackish waters, ponds, river mouths, but readily form freshwater populations. Feed on insects and fishes. Spawn during late spring or early summer in fresh or brackish water. Respond

to baits such as worms and minnows, as well as to wet and dry flies. Believed to have moved from the Mohawk-Hudson river system, through the Erie Barge Canal and Oswego R., to L. Ontario and thence to the St. Lawrence R. and L. Erie.

Striped bass
Bar rayé
Morone saxatilis **(Walbaum)**
Differ: from the white perch and white bass in their usually convex forehead and rounder, more slender body. Lower jaw projects. Have about seven dark stripes on sides and teeth on base of the tongue.
Size: to 125 lb. and over 6 ft. (North Carolina). The angling record is 60 in. and 73 lb. (Massachusetts). One 75 lb. was taken in the Saint John River, N.B., and one about 50 lb. in Grand L., N.S. Usually 4-12 lb.
Notes: live in coastal waters, adjacent rivers, and lakes. Feed on fish, crustaceans, worms, and molluscs. Spawn in

turbulent currents of brackish estuaries or in fresh water of rivers in June and July. Caught by spinning, fly fishing, and trolling. A powerful fish, obliging the angler to make full use of the play in his rod.

Sunfish family
Famille des achigans
Centrarchidae

The sunfish family is indigenous to North America. Members of the sunfish family may be recognized by the following features. The spiny and soft parts of the dorsal fin are always united at least at the base, and never form two separate fins. There are three or more sharp spines in the anal fin and there is never a spine on the operculum. The snout and the caudal fin are never rounded as in the freshwater drum.

Ten species of this family found in Canada are of interest to sport fishermen. They are predominantly fish of warmer waters, not extending very far north. All spawn in spring or summer and the males guard the eggs and young. On light tackle the smaller members are very good sport fish, particularly for younger anglers.

Plate 6

3 Anal spines

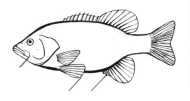

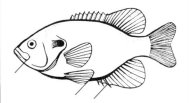

Black basses — *Micropterus*, see p.52
· Jaw long — to or past mid-eye
· Pelvic fin reaches only half-
  way to anal fin
· Body slender

Sunfishes — *Lepomis*, see pp. 50 – 51
· Jaw short — not or just to mid-eye
· Pelvics about reach anal fin
· Body deep

5–7 Anal spines

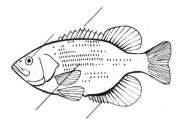

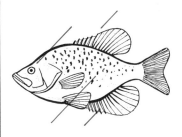

Rock basses — *Ambloplites*, see p. 54
· Red eye
· Scale spots form level rows
· Middle dorsal spine the highest
· Anal shorter than dorsal fin

Crappies — *Pomoxis*, see p. 53
· Eye not red
· Scale spots not in level rows
· Last dorsal spine the highest
· Anal as long as the dorsal fin

Pictorial Key to Genera of Sunfish Family

Bluegill
Crapet arlequin
Lepomis macrochirus **Rafinesque,**
col. pl. 11-A
Differ: from other sunfishes in the short
jaw rarely reaching the eye, the all-black,
short and flexible opercular flap, the
long pointed pectoral fin, and the dusky
spot at the end of the soft dorsal fin.
Gill rakers long.

Size: to 15 in. and 4 lb. 12 oz. — largest
caught and angling record (Alabama).
Reported to attain 10-12 in. in the Rideau
district, Ontario.
Notes: live in warm, vegetated, still
waters. Feed on insects and vegetation.
Spawn in spring and summer, the male
making a nest on sand or gravel, guarding the eggs and newly hatched young.
Will take flies, poppers, worm and insect
baits. Hybrids between the bluegill and
pumpkinseed occur. The hybrids have a
mixture of characters of both parents.

Pumpkinseed
Crapet-soleil
Lepomis gibbosus **(Linnaeus),**
col. pl. 11-B
Differ: from other sunfishes in the short
jaw not passing front of eye, in the red
spot on end of the short stiff opercular
flap, in the short pointed pectoral fin
and in the spotted soft dorsal. Gill rakers
short.
Size: to 12 in. and 17 oz. One of 9½ in.
fork length was caught in Borstein's Bay,

St. Lawrence R., Ont.
Notes: live in clear, shallow, vegetated
waters — ponds, lakes, or streams. Feed
on insects and snails. Spawn in June or
July, the male making a nest, guarding
the eggs and newly hatched fry. The
bright colours and eager biting of this
fish start many youngsters on a life of
angling. Flies, floating "bug" lures, or
grasshoppers and worms on small hooks
are attractive to this brightly coloured
fish.

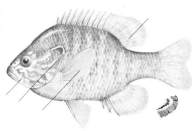

Longear sunfish
Crapet à longues oreilles
Lepomis megalotis (Rafinesque)

Differ: from other sunfishes in the moderate jaw which extends past the front of the eye; in the moderate to long, light-bordered, red-tipped, and flexible opercular lobe; in the moderately long, rounded pectoral fin; and in the dorsal fin without definite dark spots. Gill rakers very short. Reach about 6 in. Not common, occur in southern and western Ontario and in southern Quebec.

Green sunfish
Crapet vert

Lepomis cyanellus Rafinesque

Differ: from other sunfishes in the long jaw extending past front of eye; in the light-bordered, stiff, short opercular flap; in the short round pectoral fin; and in the dusky spot at the base of the end of the dorsal fin. Gill rakers long. Attain 12 in. and 2 lb. 2 oz. (Kansas). Not common, occur in southern and northwestern Ontario, there reaching 5 in.

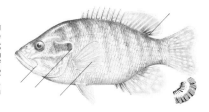

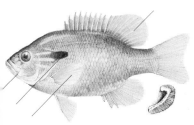

Redbreast sunfish
Crapet rouge
Lepomis auritus (Linnaeus),
col. pl. 11-C

Differ: from other sunfishes in the moderate jaw reaching just to eye; in the all-dark, flexible, long opercular flap; in the short round pectoral fin; and in the dorsal fin without definite dark spots. Gill rakers short. Reach 9.4 in. Occur in New Brunswick, there reaching 7 in.

Smallmouth bass
Achigan à petite bouche
Micropterus dolomieui Lacépède,
col. pl. 12-A

Differ: from largemouth in the short upper jaw seldom reaching behind the eye, the rounded outline of the first dorsal, the high dark vertical bars on sides, and the scales on membrane of the base of anal and second dorsal fins.
Size: to 27 in. and 11 lb. 15 oz. — the angling record and largest caught (Tennessee). One of 24 in. and 9 lb. 13½ oz. was caught in Birch L. near Kinmount, Ont., by A. Anderson in 1951, and another one of 11 lb. 6 oz. in Ontario in 1960. Usually 1½ to 2½ lb.
Notes: live in hard-bottomed streams and large lakes, preferring those with clear water, little vegetation, and gravel or rock bottoms. Feed on fishes, crayfishes and insects. Spawn from May to July, the male making a saucer-shaped hollow on a gravel, sand, or rocky bottom, fertilizing the eggs, then guarding the eggs and fry. Taken on artificial lures and flies or bait, they provide a vigorous challenge to the angler.

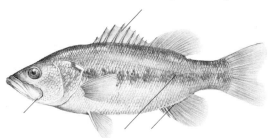

Largemouth bass
Achigan à grande bouche
Micropterus salmoides (Lacépède),
col. pls. 12-B, 12-C

Differ: from smallmouth in the long upper jaw extending well past the hind edge of the eye, the triangular outline of the first dorsal, the dark horizontal band along the side, the absence of scales on the bases of anal and second dorsal fins.
Size: to 32½ in. and 22 lb. 4 oz. — the angling record and largest caught (Georgia). One of 28 in. and 14 lb. 2 oz. was caught by L. Noonan at McCracken's Landing, Stoney L., Ont., in July 1948. Usually 2-3 lb.
Notes: live in slow or still waters of warm lakes and streams, preferring those that are weedy and mud-bottomed. Feed predominantly on fish but also consume crayfish and frogs. Spawn from May to June, the male behaving as in the smallmouth, but building the nest on soft bottom. A wide variety of surface lures, flies, and baits cast from shore or boats attract the largemouth. Early morning and evening are considered the most productive times.

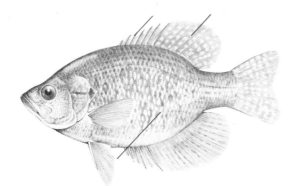

Black crappie
Marigane noire
***Pomoxis nigromaculatus* (Lesueur),**
col. pl. 13-A
Differ: from white crappie in having 7-8 dorsal spines, dorsal fin base longer than head length, spotting on sides not in vertical bands, and body deeper.
Size: to 19¼ in. and 5 lb. — largest caught and angling record (South Carolina). One of 11.2 in. fork length and 1 lb. 3 oz. was angled in Rideau L., Ont. Usually 7-10 in. and ½ lb.
Notes: live in clear weedy lakes and slow streams. Often form schools. Feed on small fishes, insects, and crustaceans. Spawn in May and June in or near vege-

tation. The males guard the eggs and young. Bait such as small live minnows, small flies, and lures such as fly rod poppers on long fine leaders are effective.

White crappie
Marigane blanche
***Pomoxis annularis* Rafinesque,**
col. pl. 13-B
Differ: from black crappie in having 5-6 dorsal spines, dorsal fin base shorter than head length, spotting forming vertical bands on sides, and body less deep. The largest caught and the angling record is one of 6 lb. (Louisiana). Usually 7-10 in. Occur in southern Ontario, but rarely caught.

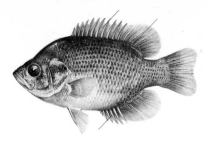 

Rock bass
Crapet de roche
Ambloplites rupestris **(Rafinesque)**
Differ: from others in the family in having 11-12 dorsal spines, 5-7 anal spines, and dark spots forming horizontal rows on the scales.
Size: to 3 lb. 10 oz. (Michigan) but usually 6-8 in. and ½ lb.

Notes: live in warm, clear, slow waters of streams and lakes with boulder, gravel, or bedrock bottom. Feed on insects, crayfish, and small fish. Spawn in June. Eggs and young are guarded by the male. Bite on flies, bass bugs, spinning lures, as well as various baits such as minnows, grasshoppers and worms. A spunky fish on light tackle. Its taste warrants more frequent use at the table.

Perch family
Famille des perches
Percidae

The perch family occurs in the fresh waters of North America and Eurasia. The perches, unlike the sunfish family, have two well-separated dorsal fins; unlike the temperate basses they lack opercular spines. There are only two weak spines in the anal, whereas in the sunfishes and temperate basses there are three or more strong sharp spines.

There are over a dozen species of the perch family in Canada, but only three are sought by the sportsman. The remaining species are the darters, which are tiny, slender and often brilliantly coloured. They rest on the bottom, darting forward now and then to seize a minute morsel of food.

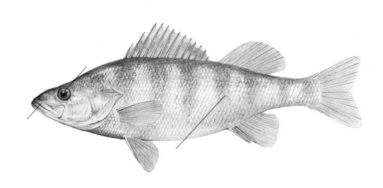

Yellow perch
Perchaude
Perca fluviatilis Linnaeus

Differ: from walleye and sauger in lacking canine teeth, in having clear eyes, and in having narrow, dark, vertical bars on sides.

Size: to 4 lb. 3½ oz. — the angling record and largest caught (New Jersey). Lengths up to at least 13½ in. are reached. One 4 lb. 1 oz. was angled in Quebec by R. Labelle in 1957. Usually about ½ lb. although the "jumbo" perch caught in spring in L. Simcoe, Ont., are larger.

Notes: live in clear waters of lakes, ponds and slow streams where there is some vegetation. Often school. Feed on insects, crayfish, snails, and fish. Spawn in April and May, laying jelly-like bands of eggs in shallow water. May be caught on worms or minnows, flies or spinners fished near the bottom in open water or through the ice. A favourite fish of old and young in summer and winter.

Sauger
Doré noir
Stizostedion canadense (Smith),
col. pl. 14-B

Differ: from the walleye in the fully-scaled cheeks, in having rows of black spots in the first dorsal fin, in having 17-19 rays in the second dorsal fin and 5-9 pyloric caeca. From the perch differ in having canine teeth, a more slender body, and smoky eyes, and in lacking narrow vertical bands.

Size: 8 lb. 6 oz. — the angling record and largest caught (North Dakota). One 19 in. fork length was caught in the Milk R., Alberta, in 1966 by T. Willock. Usually about 1 lb. and 12-14 in.

Notes: live in lakes and in slow and somewhat silty rivers. Feed on fishes, insects, and freshwater shrimps. Spawn in spring. Caught by trolling, casting, or still fishing with live bait or lures. Night fishing, when they move into shallow water, is often effective.

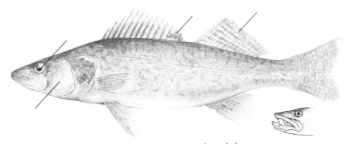

Walleye
Doré jaune
Stizostedion vitreum (Mitchill),
col. pl. 14-A

Differ: from sauger in the smooth or sparsely scaled cheeks, in having only one black spot at the end of the first dorsal fin, in having 20-22 rays in the second dorsal fin and only three pyloric caeca. From the perch in having canine teeth, a more slender body and smoky eyes, and in lacking vertical bands.

Size: to 41 in. and 25 lb. — the world angling record and largest caught (Tennessee). One 23 lb. 9 oz. was netted in the Moon R., Parry Sound District, Ont. Usually 2-3 lb.

Notes: live in cold clear waters of rivers and lakes and are more active at night. Often school. Feed mainly on fish. Spawn in streams (or lakes) on sand or gravel bottom after break-up. Trolled or cast lures or bright flies, and baits like minnows, are effective. Usually called pickerel or pike-perch in Canada, but the name "pickerel" properly indicates small species of the pike family. An ice-blue subspecies, the blue walleye, occurred in Lake Erie and Lake Ontario but now is apparently extinct. The typical subspecies, the yellow walleye, is brassy yellow, or occasionally dull grey. The dull grey form often thought to be blue walleye.

Drum family
Famille des tambours
Sciaenidae

The freshwater drum is restricted to the fresh waters of North America, although most members of the family are marine. Its rounded snout, rounded caudal fin, and long stout second anal spine distinguish it from other fishes. There is no spine on the operculum.

The freshwater drum is capable of making a purring or a grunting sound. The large, circular otoliths or ear bones, bearing an "L" on one face, are known as lucky stones. The pharyngeal bones bear pebble-like teeth; these are used in crushing their molluscan food.

Although now seldom surpassing 20 lb., specimens approaching 100 lb. were reported in early days. Bones found at Indian archaeological sites suggest that weights of 200 lb. may have been attained in prehistoric times.

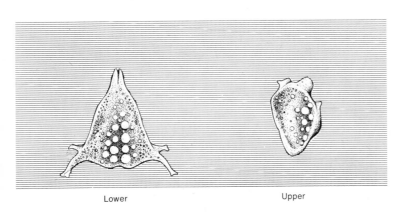

Lower   Upper

Pharyngeal teeth

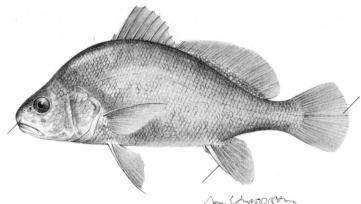

Freshwater drum
Malachigan
Aplodinotus grunniens **Rafinesque,**
col. pl. 15

Differ: from other fishes in having a rounded snout, the second anal spine long and stout, and a rounded caudal fin.

Size: to 60 lb. and a length of at least 39 in. One of 26 lb. was angled from the Whitemud R., Man., by Lloyd Drayson in 1956. Usually 1-2 lb.

Notes: Live in shallow waters of lakes and larger rivers, preferring mud or sandy bottoms. Feed on bottom, taking molluscs, crayfishes, fish and insects. Spawn in spring or early summer. Reach at least 12 years of age. Will take live bait such as crayfish, worms or minnows fished on or near the bottom.

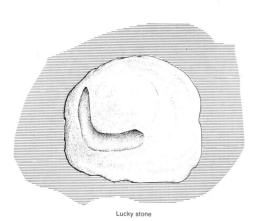

Lucky stone

APPENDICES

Making Fish Prints
Knots
Preparing Fish
Other Information Useful to the Angler

MAKING FISH PRINTS

Japanese anglers have an elegant method of recording their catch, by making a print from the fish itself. They call it *gyo-taku*. To make one yourself, first wipe the side of the fish clean and dry. Apply black liquid carbon ink with a brush or cloth to the head, body, and fins of the fish, covering the whole side and spreading it evenly. Japanese "sumi" ink employed in brush writing is ideal, but other inks, poster-paint or thinned oil paint can be used. (Don't use toxic lead base paints if you plan to eat this fish.)

Stretch a piece of absorptive paper and lower it down onto the fish. Rice paper of the type used for shoji screens is traditional but substitutes that take ink will do. Do not shift the paper or a double image will result. Hold the paper in position and rub the paper where it contacts the body of the fish. Spread the fins with one hand and press the paper down on them with the other. Then peel the finished print off. Several prints can be made. The fish can then be washed and eaten.

The place, date, species and size can be added. Finer prints are well worth framing. By adding extra ink to the fish's back the effect of shading can be achieved. One can even use colour. An elegant permanent record of the form and size of your catch results.

References

Anonymous. 1966. How to imprint a trophy fish. *Wildlife Review* 3(9): 8-9, illus.

Hiyama, Yoshio. 1964. *Gyotaku, fish print. What is it? How to make it?* Tokyo, University of Tokyo Press, 64 pp., illus. $5.40. (Obtainable from Yurin-sha Ltd., P.O. Box 398, Tokyo Central, Tokyo, Japan.)

KNOTS

A good knot may save a lure, a fish, or a boat. The following figures divide the tying of each knot into two or three simple steps. Arrows indicate the end to pull to tighten the knot. Angling knots are included for tying line to hooks, making loops, tying two lines together, and whipping a rod. The *towing hitch* for towing boats can be quickly undone if necessary. The *bowline* is useful for tying up a boat. A bit of practice on a rainy day will give you dependable friends that will serve you the rest of your life.

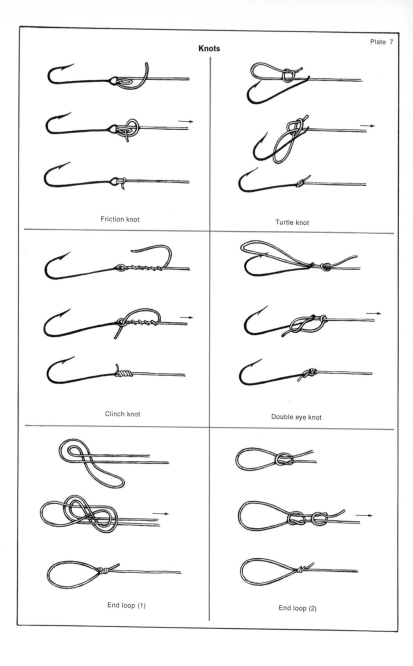

Knots

Plate 7

Friction knot

Turtle knot

Clinch knot

Double eye knot

End loop (1)

End loop (2)

Plate 8

Knots

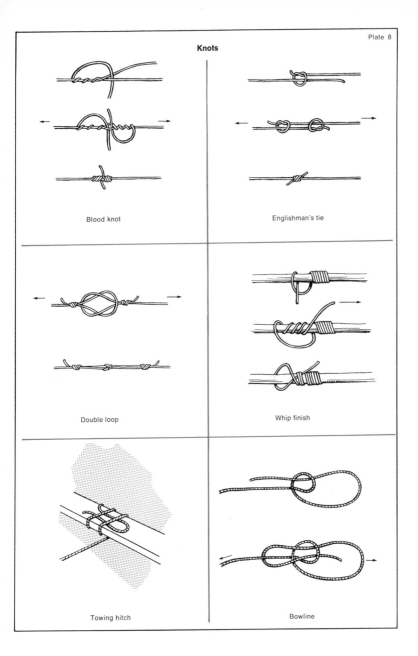

Blood knot

Englishman's tie

Double loop

Whip finish

Towing hitch

Bowline

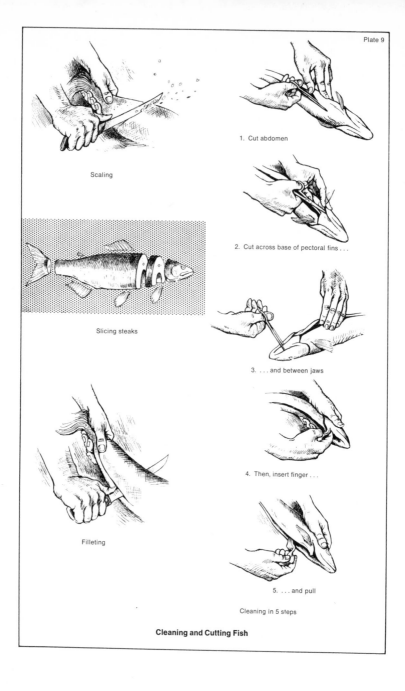

Plate 9

Scaling

1. Cut abdomen

2. Cut across base of pectoral fins . . .

Slicing steaks

3. . . . and between jaws

4. Then, insert finger . . .

Filleting

5. . . . and pull

Cleaning in 5 steps

Cleaning and Cutting Fish

PREPARING FISH

The following recipes, taken from the sources cited at the end of this section, are quoted through the kindness of Miss Margaret Myers, Consumer Section, Fisheries Service, Department of the Environment. A variety are given, with simple ones for campers and some fancy ones for use on cabin cruisers or at home. *See* the following figures for cleaning and cutting fish; *see also* the references for further recipes as well as directions on preparing, storing and freezing fish. Over 50,000 copies of the *Canadian Fish Cook Book* have been sold.

Recipes

Grilled Fish in Foil

2 pounds fish fillets	1 teaspoon salt
6 green pepper rings	¼ teaspoon pepper
6 thin onion slices	1 tablespoon butter or other fat

Cut fillets into serving-size pieces. Top each serving with a ring of green pepper and a slice of onion. Season with salt and pepper; dot with fat. Package each serving in a steam-tight envelope of greased heavy aluminum foil. Place foil packages directly on hot coals and cook about 10 minutes or until the fish flakes easily when tested with a fork. The fish may be served in the packages. Makes 6 servings.

Pan-fried Perch Fillets

2 pounds perch fillets
½ cup milk
½ teaspoon salt
⅛ teaspoon pepper
½ teaspoon poultry seasoning
½ cup flour

Dip fish in milk and then in seasoned flour. Fry in about ¼-inch hot fat until brown on one side; turn and brown the other side. Allow about 3 or 4 minutes cooking on each side. Makes 6 servings.

Wine-poached Trout

2 or 3 rainbow trout
¼ teaspoon dill seeds
¼ teaspoon rosemary
⅛ teaspoon seasoning salt
½ cup dry white wine
salad greens

Clean trout and remove heads, tails and fins. Add seasoning to wine and poach trout for 15 to 20 minutes or until done. Allow fish to cool in poaching liquid. Remove skin and lift fillets from bones. Serve trout on crisp salad greens with the following mayonnaise dressing:

½ cup mayonnaise
2 tablespoons chopped green onions
2 teaspoons chopped pimiento
2 teaspoons chopped dill pickles

Combine all ingredients. Makes 2 to 3 servings.

Fish Fry

6 perch or other small fish
½ cup cornmeal
½ cup flour
1 tablespoon salt

Clean and scale perch. Cut off heads. Dip in water, then coat with mixture of cornmeal, flour and salt. Fry in about ¼-inch hot fat until cooked, turning to brown both sides. Cook for about 6 minutes or until fish flakes easily when tested with a fork. Makes 6 servings.

Baked Walleye Fillets

2 pounds walleye fillets
½ cup milk
1 teaspoon salt
½ cup fine dry bread crumbs
2 tablespoons butter or other fat

Cut fillets into serving-size portions and soak three minutes in milk to which salt has been added. Drain and roll in bread crumbs. Place fish in greased baking dish and dot with fat. Measure thickness of fish. Bake in hot oven (450°F). Allow 10 minutes cooking time for each inch of thickness. If fish is frozen, double the cooking time. Makes 6 servings.

Parmesan Smelt

2 pounds smelt
½ cup flour
½ teaspoon salt
⅛ teaspoon pepper
1 egg, beaten
1 tablespoon lemon juice
½ cup cracker crumbs
⅓ cup grated Parmesan cheese

Clean and bone smelt. Combine flour, salt and pepper. Coat fish with mixture. Dip fish in combined egg and lemon juice. Roll in mixed cracker crumbs and cheese. Pan-fry in about ¼ inch of hot fat. When golden brown on one side, turn and brown the other side. Makes 6 servings.

Smoking Fish

Smoked fish is one of the most delicious of foods. Smoking is also a useful method of preserving one's catch and preventing spoilage when fishing in remote areas. A simple design for smokehouses is shown following this section. Either of the following two curing compounds may be used:

Curing Mixture 1
4 cups of salt
2 cups of brown sugar
2 tablespoons of black pepper
2 tablespoons of bay leaves
    (1 gallon of water may be added
    to make it into a curing brine 1)

Curing Brine 2
1 gallon fresh cold water
4 cups of salt

Step 1
Slit fresh fish; remove guts, gills and backbone; do not skin or scale.

Step 2a
Dry method – rub on dry curing mixture 1 (recommended by the authors).

or

Step 2b
Brine-dip method – leave fish in curing brine 1 or 2. For average-sized fish about 1 hour (more if salty taste desired). Then drain excess fluid off fish and allow to dry until glazed (shiny appearance of dried brine) 2-3 hours.

Step 3
Start smokehouse. Burn hardwood sawdust or small pieces of wood. Use green alder, willow or poplar; dry beech, oak, or hickory; birch without bark. Even sphagnum will do. Avoid wood of conifers.

Step 4
Place metal hooks under gill covers and hang on rods in smokehouse or lay skin side down on screen or rod shelves in smokehouse.

Step 5
Check fuel and smoke volume every 2-3 hours.

Step 6a
"Barbecuing method" – smoke 8-10 hours with smokehouse hot (over 110°F). These fish will not keep over five days without refrigeration, but are tastier.

or

Step 6b
"Slow smoke method" – smoke for several days at lower temperatures. These drier fish will keep much longer without refrigeration and are stronger in smoke flavour.

Step 7
When done, the flesh should be golden brown to copper brown and look dry on surface. Flavour may be taste-tested to determine end point.

Step 8
Wrap fish in wax paper or aluminum foil. Refrigerate or freeze if necessary.

Smokehouse

References

Canada, Department of the Environment. 1969. *Canadian fish cook book*. (Ottawa, Queen's Printer), 96 pp., illus. $1.50.

Canada, Department of the Environment. 1970. *Let's serve freshwater fish*. (Ottawa, Queen's Printer), 32 pp. (Free on individual request.)

Jarvis, Norman J. 1950. *Curing of fishery products*. United States Fish and Wildlife Service, Research Report (18): 1-271, illus.

Lantz, A. W. 1964. *A practical method for brining and smoking fish*. Reprinted from June 1964 *Trade News,* Department of the Environment, 4 pp., illus.

Marécat, Claire. 1972. *Le poisson dans la cuisine québécoise*. Montreal, Editions La Presse, 143 pp., illus. $3.00.

OTHER INFORMATION USEFUL TO THE ANGLER

For the devotee, we have included sources of further information on various aspects of angling. The emphasis has been placed on Canadian sources. As may be guessed from publication dates, some of the books are out of print and only second-hand copies may be obtained. Publications of the Canadian government are available at government book shops in Vancouver, Winnipeg, Toronto, Ottawa, Montreal and Halifax, through your local bookseller or by writing to Information Canada, Ottawa.

Books and Periodicals on Fishes

The following publications may be of assistance in identifying fishes and learning more about their life histories. Books dealing with marine fishes are also included.

• On Major Regions of Canada

The works below cover two or more provinces or territories:

American Fisheries Society. 1970. *A list of common and scientific names of fishes from the United States and Canada.* 2nd ed. American Fisheries Society Special Publication (2): 1-102, $1.50. (Obtainable from Secretary, American Fisheries Society, 1404 New York Ave., N.W., Washington, D.C.)

Leim, A.H., and W.B. Scott. 1966. *Fishes of the Atlantic coast of Canada.* Fisheries Research Board of Canada, Bulletin (155): 1-485, illus. $8.50.

McAllister, D.E. 1960. *List of the marine fishes of Canada.* National Museum of Canada, Bulletin (168): 1-76. $1.25.

———. 1960. *Key to the marine fishes of Arctic Canada.* National Museum of Canada, Natural History Papers (5): 1-21, illus.

McPhail, J.D., and C.C. Lindsey. 1970. *Freshwater fishes of northwestern Canada and Alaska.* Fisheries Research Board of Canada, Bulletin (173): 1-381, illus. $8.50.

Scott, W. B. 1967. *Freshwater fishes of eastern Canada.* 2nd ed. Toronto, University of Toronto Press, 137 pp., photos. $2.25. (Obtainable from your bookstore or the publisher.)

———, and E. J. Crossman. 1969. *Checklist and keys to Canadian freshwater fishes.* Royal Ontario Museum, Miscellaneous Publication. 104 pp.

———. In press. *Freshwater fishes of Canada.* Fisheries Research Board of Canada, Bulletin (184): 1-952, illus. $9.75.

———, and M. G. Scott. 1965. *A checklist of Canadian Atlantic fishes with keys for identification.* Royal Ontario Museum, Life Sciences Contribution (66): 1-106, 2 fig.

Sears Foundation for Marine Research, Memoirs, 1953 to present. *Fishes of the western north Atlantic.* New Haven, Yale University. $27.50 a part. (A series still to be completed; pts. 1-5 published.)

• On the Provinces

The following publications deal with the fish fauna at the provincial level. The National Parks Service, Ottawa, and some provincial parks services have, in addition, small pamphlets on fishes of their parks. The publications are listed in order of the provinces from west to east.

British Columbia

Carl, G. C., W. A. Clemens, and C. C. Lindsey. 1967. *The fresh-water fishes of British Columbia.* 4th ed. British Columbia Provincial Museum Handbook (5): 1-192, illus. 75¢. (Obtainable from the Provincial Museum of Natural History and Anthropology, Victoria, B.C.)

Hart, J.L. 1973. *Pacific fishes.* 2nd ed. Fisheries Research Board of Canada, Bulletin (180): 1-668, illus. $8.00.

Alberta

Hardy, W. G., ed. 1967. *Alberta: a natural history.* Edmonton, Hurtig, 343 pp., illus. ("The angler's domain" by M. J. Paetz, pp. 248-255.)

MacDonald, W. H. 1951. *Fishing in Alberta.* Alberta Travel Bureau. Edmonton, King's Printer for Alberta, 36 pp., illus.

Paetz, Martin J., and Joseph S. Nelson. 1970. *The fishes of Alberta.* Edmonton, Queen's Printer, 282 pp., illus., $6.00.

Saskatchewan

Symington, D. F. 1959. *The fish of Saskatchewan.* Saskatchewan Dept. of Natural Resources, Conservation Bulletin (7): 1-25, illus.

Manitoba

Fedoruk, Alex N. 1969. *Checklist and key of the freshwater fishes of Manitoba.* Winnipeg, Manitoba Department of Mines and Natural Resources, Canada Land Inventory Project, 98 pp., illus.

Hinks, David. 1943. *The fishes of Manitoba.* Winnipeg, Manitoba Department of Mines and Natural Resources, 102 pp., illus.

Keleher, J. J., and B. Kooyman. 1957. *Supplement to Hink's "The fishes of Manitoba."* Winnipeg, Manitoba Department of Mines and Natural Resources, pp. 104-107.

Ontario

Hubbs, C. L., and K. F. Lagler. 1964. *Fishes of the Great Lakes region.* Cranbrook Institute of Science Bulletin (26): 1-213, illus.

MacKay, H. H. 1963. *Fishes of Ontario.* Toronto, Ontario Department of Lands and Forests, 360 pp., illus.

Quebec

Juchereau-Duchesnay, E. 1956. *Les poissons de chez nous.* Le Club de pêche Molson. 85 pp., illus.

———. 1964 *Les poissons du Québec.* Montreal, Les Editions de l'Homme, 47 pp., illus.

Legendre, Vianney. 1954. *Key to game and commercial fishes of the province of Quebec.* 1st English ed. Quebec, Department of Game and Fisheries, 189 pp., illus.

Melançon, Claude. 1958. *Les poissons de nos eaux.* 3rd ed. Quebec, La Société zoologique de Québec, 254 pp., illus.

Quebec, Department of Tourism, Fish and Game. 1970. *La pêche sportive au Québec/Sportfishing in Quebec.* 52 pp., illus. Bilingual. (Obtainable from the Tourist Branch, 12 Ste-Anne Street, Quebec.)

New Brunswick

Scott, W. B., and E. J. Crossman. 1959. *The freshwater fishes of New Brunswick: A checklist with distributional notes.* Royal Ontario Museum, Div. of Zoology and Palaeontology, Contribution (51): 1-37.

Gorham, S. W. 1970. *Distributional checklist of the fishes of New Brunswick.* Saint John, New Brunswick, 32 pp.

Nova Scotia

Livingstone, D. A. 1951. *The freshwater fishes of Nova Scotia.* Nova Scotian Institute of Science, Proceedings 23: 1-90, illus.

Vladykov, V. D., and R. A. McKenzie. 1936. *The marine fishes of Nova Scotia.* Nova Scotian Institute of Science, Proceedings 19: 17-113, illus.

Newfoundland

Scott, W. B., and E. J. Crossman. 1964. *Fishes occurring in the fresh waters of insular Newfoundland.* Canada, Department of Fisheries and Forestry. Ottawa, Queen's Printer. 124 pp., illus. $4.00.

- Books on Angling

Bennett, Tiny. 1970. *The art of angling.* Scarborough, Ont., Prentice Hall, 288 pp., illus.

Canadian Government Travel Bureau. 1968. *Canada, fisherman's paradise.* Ottawa, Queen's Printer, 31 pp., illus.

Chamberland, Michel. 1966. *La pêche au Québec.* Montreal, Editions de l'Homme, 350 pp., illus.

Deyglun, Serge. 1972. *La pêche sportive au Québec,* Montreal, Editions du Jour, 267 pp., illus., colour plates.

Haig-Brown, Roderick L. 1947. *The western angler; an account of Pacific salmon and western trout in British Columbia.* New York, William Morrow, 356 pp., illus.

———. 1949. *On the highest hill.* New York, William Morrow, 319 pp.

———. 1950. *Measure of the year.* Toronto, William Collins, 260 pp.

———. 1951. *Fisherman's spring.* Toronto, William Collins, 222 pp., illus.

———. 1954. *Fisherman's winter.* New York, William Morrow, 288 pp., illus.

———. 1959. *Fisherman's summer.* Toronto, William Collins, 253 pp., illus.

———. 1964. *A primer of fly-fishing.* New York, William Morrow, 189 pp., illus.

———. 1964. *Fisherman's fall.* Toronto, William Collins, 279 pp.

Whitehouse, Francis C. 1946. *Sport fishes of western Canada and some others.* Toronto, McClelland and Stewart, 129 pp., illus.

Wooding, F. H. 1959. *The angler's book of Canadian fishes.* Don Mills, Ont., Collins, 303 pp., illus.

- Mounting and Preserving Fishes

Anderson, R. M. 1965. *Methods of collecting and preserving vertebrate animals.* (Information on scientific specimens of fishes in chap. VI.) National Museum of Canada, Bulletin (69): 1-199, illus. Ottawa, Queen's Printer, $2.00.

Migdalski, Edward C. 1960. *How to make fish mounts and other fish trophies.* New York, Ronald Press, 218 pp., illus.

- General Ichthyological Texts

Alexander, R. McN. 1967. *Functional design in fishes.* London, Biological Sciences, Hutchinson University Library, 160 pp., illus.

Grassé, Pierre P. 1958. *Agnathes et poissons, anatomie, éthologie, systématique.* Traité de Zoologie, vol. 13, 3 pts. Paris, Masson, 2758 pp., illus.

Lagler, K. F. 1956. *Freshwater fishery biology.* Dubuque, Iowa, Wm. C. Brown, 421 pp., illus.

—————, J. E. Bardach, and R. R. Miller. 1962. *Ichthyology.* New York, John Wiley, 545 pp., illus.

Marshall, N. B. 1965. *The life of fishes.* London, Weidenfeld and Nicolson, 402 pp., illus.

————— . 1971. *Explorations in the life of fishes.* Harvard Books in Biology, No. 7. Cambridge, Mass., Harvard University Press, 204 pp., illus.

Norman, J. R., and P. H. Greenwood. 1963. *A history of fishes.* 2nd ed. London, Ernest Benn, 398 pp.

————— . 1950. *Nouvelle histoire naturelle des poissons.* Trans. and ed. E. Le Danois. Paris, Payot, 353 pp., illus.

Vibert, R., and K. F. Lagler. 1961. *Pêches continentales.* Paris, Dunod, 270 pp., illus.

- On the Water and Its Life

Frey, David G. 1963. *Limnology in North America.* Madison, University of Wisconsin Press, 734 pp., illus.

Macan, T. T., and E. B. Worthington. 1951. *Life in lakes and rivers.* London, William Collins, 272 pp., illus.

Needham, J. G., and P. R. Needham. 1955. *A guide to the study of freshwater biology.* Ithaca, N.Y., Comstock, 88 pp., illus.

Welch, Paul S. 1952. *Limnology.* 2nd ed. New York, McGraw Hill, 536 pp., illus.

- Periodicals

Actualités marines. Quebec, Department of Tourism, Fish and Game. Quarterly.

The Atlantic Salmon Journal. Montreal, Atlantic Salmon Association. Quarterly.

Au Grand Air. Montreal, Rod & Gun Pub. Corp. Bimonthly.

Bulletin Tourism, Fish and Game/Bulletin Tourisme, Chasse et Pêche. Quebec, Department of Tourism, Fish and Game. Every two months. Bilingual.

The Canadian Fish Culturist. Department of the Environment. Ottawa, Information Canada.

Fish and Game. Calgary.

Fisheries of Canada. Department of the Environment. Ottawa. Monthly.

Hunting and Fishing in Canada. Toronto, Jardine & Young Ltd. Monthly.

Land, Forest, Wildlife. Edmonton, Alberta Department of Lands and Forests.

Newsletter. Ottawa, Canadian Wildlife Federation.

Northern Sportsman. Fort Frances, Ont., Fort Frances Times Ltd.

Ontario Fish and Wildlife Review. Toronto, Ontario Ministry of Natural Resources.

Rod & Gun in Canada. Montreal, Rod & Gun Pub. Corp. Monthly.

Western Fish and Game. West Vancouver, B. C., Box 303. Bimonthly.

Wildlife Review. Victoria, Fish and Wildlife Branch, British Columbia Department of Recreation and Conservation. Quarterly.

Provincial Anglers' Associations

British Columbia Federation of Fish and Game Clubs, 4330 Dominion Street, Burnaby, B.C.

Alberta Fish and Game Association, Room 212, 8631-109th Street, Edmonton.

Saskatchewan Fish and Game League, 1122 Temperance Street, Saskatoon.

Manitoba Federation of Game and Fish Associations, MacIntyre Building, Winnipeg.

Ontario Federation of Anglers and Hunters, Suite 204, Lowrie Building, 15 Yonge Street N., Richmond Hill.

Quebec Federation of Fish and Game Associations, 1600 Berri Street, Suite 210, Montreal.

Prince Edward Island Fish and Game Association, Summerside.

Nova Scotia Fish and Game Association, P. O. Box 654, Halifax.

Fishing Licences and Regulations

The federal government administers all tidal fisheries except those of Quebec. It also administers completely or in part the freshwater fisheries of the Yukon, Northwest Territories, Nova Scotia, New Brunswick, Prince Edward Island, and Newfoundland. The remaining provinces administer their own freshwater fisheries. Fisheries of the National Parks of Canada are administered by the National Parks Service of the Department of Indian and Northern Affairs, Ottawa. For information write the following, listed in order from west to east:

Yukon Territory: Fisheries Service, Department of the Environment, Box 2410, Whitehorse.

British Columbia: *freshwater* — Fish and Game Branch, Department of Recreation and Conservation, Parliament Buildings, Victoria; *tidal* — Director, Fisheries Service, Department of the Environment, 1155 Robson Street, Vancouver 5.

Northwest Territories: Travel Arctic, Yellowknife.

Alberta: Director, Fish and Wildlife Division, Department of Lands and Forests, Edmonton.

Saskatchewan: Saskatchewan Tourist Bureau, Regina.

Manitoba: Director of Fisheries, Department of Mines and Natural Resources, 910 Norquay Building, Winnipeg 1.

Ontario: Chief, Sport Fishery Branch, Ontario Ministry of Natural Resources, Parliament Buildings, Toronto 5.

Quebec: Inspector General of the Protection Service, Department of Tourism, Fish and Game, Parliament Buildings, Quebec City.

New Brunswick: Fish and Wildlife Branch, Department of Natural Resources, Fredericton.

Prince Edward Island: P.E.I. Department of Fisheries, Fish and Wildlife Division, P.O. Box 2000, Charlottetown.

Nova Scotia: Nova Scotia Department of Lands and Forests, P.O. Box 699, Halifax, or Federal Building, Bedford Row, Halifax.

Newfoundland: *freshwater* — Director of Fishing and Hunting Development, Department of Mines, Agriculture and Resources, St. John's; *tidal* — Area Director, Fisheries Service, Department of the Environment, St. John's.

Travel and Maps

For travel and tourist information write: Canadian Government Travel Bureau, 150 Kent Street, Ottawa 4, or individual provinces as below. The Travel Bureau publishes *Where to Fish in Canada.*

For national topographic maps, aeronautical charts, magnetic maps and general maps write: Map Distribution Office, Ottawa 4.

For geological maps write: Geological Survey of Canada, 601 Booth Street, Ottawa, Ont. K1A 0E8.

For nautical charts, pilots, tide tables, and publications relating to navigation write: Marine Sciences Branch, Canadian Hydrographic Service, 615 Booth Street, Ottawa, Ont. K1A 0E9.

For air photos write: National Air Photo Library, 615 Booth Street, Ottawa, Ont. K1A 0E9.

For travel and tourist information on the provinces write the following departments or agencies:

Yukon Territory: Yukon Territory, Department of Travel and Publicity, Box 2703, Whitehorse.

British Columbia: Department of Recreation and Conservation, Fish and Wildlife Branch, Parliament Buildings, Victoria. Publishes *British Columbia Roadmap, Campsite and Fishing Guide.*

Northwest Territories: Travel Arctic, Yellowknife, N.W.T.

Alberta: Alberta Government Travel Bureau, Room 115, Highway Building, Edmonton. Publishes annually the *Alberta Accommodation Guide* and *Alberta Angling: A Broad Picture.*

Saskatchewan: Saskatchewan Travel Bureau, Saskatchewan Power Building, Regina.

Manitoba: Tourist Branch, Department of Tourism and Recreation, 511 Norquay Building, Winnipeg 1. Publishes *Fish Manitoba* and *Manitoba Master Angler Award Winners.*

Ontario: Department of Tourism and Information, 185 Bloor Street East, Toronto 285. Publishes *Hunting and Fishing in Ontario.*

Quebec: Department of Tourism, Fish and Game, Quebec City.

New Brunswick: New Brunswick Travel Bureau, 796 Queen Street, Fredericton. Publishes *Fish and Hunt Outfitting Listings.*

Prince Edward Island: P.E.I. Travel Bureau, Charlottetown.

Nova Scotia: Nova Scotia Travel Bureau, Provincial Building, Halifax.

Newfoundland: Tourist Development Office, Confederation Building, St. John's. Publishes annually *Fishing in Newfoundland and Labrador* (and general information).

Canoeing and Boating

Owners of large yachts or users of well-travelled waterways, such as the seaway system, may obtain free of charge *Notices to Mariners* giving details of changes in charts and other data of interest to shipping. Write to: Chief, Aids to Navigation, Department of Transport, Ottawa, Ontario. Also note reference to charts above.

Canadian Government Travel Bureau. 1963. *Canoe trips in Canada.* Ottawa, Queen's Printer, 30 pp. (Canoe routes, fishing prospects, cruise outfit checklist.)

Department of Transport. 1966. *Safety afloat, for owners of pleasure boats and small commercial craft.* Ottawa, Queen's Printer, 32 pp., illus. (Distributed free of charge, published annually to provide latest information and regulations.)

─────── . 1966. *Navigation canals, Rideau, Trent, Quebec*. Bilingual. Ottawa, Queen's Printer, 10 pp. + 10 pp. of illus. (Distributed free of charge, published annually to provide latest information.)

─────── . 1966. *Canal regulations governing the use and management of the Department of Transport navigation canals*. Ottawa, Queen's Printer, 26 pp. + amendments. 35¢.

Glossary of Fish Anatomy

abdomen — the lower part of the trunk between the vent and the pectoral fins, enclosing the body cavity.

adipose — the fleshy fin on the upper edge of the body in front of the tail fin having, unlike the other fins, no supporting rays or spines.

alevin — a young fish still bearing the yolk sac.

anal fin — the fin on the lower edge of the body between the vent and tail fin.

annual rings — the bunched growth rings on a scale separating one year's growth from the next.

aquatic — relating to water.

barbel — a slender process near the mouth used as an organ of touch, taste or smell.

basibranchial teeth — the teeth behind the tongue and between the base of the gills.

branchiostegals — splint-like bones supporting the skin below the gill cover.

body cavity — the cavity containing the heart, stomach, intestines, gas bladder, kidney, etc.

canine — enlarged conical teeth.

caudal fin — the tail fin.

caudal peduncle — the wrist-like portion of the body in front of the tail fin.

cheek — area behind and below the eye and in front of the gill cover.

chromatophores — the small cells that give colour to the skin.

crustaceans — a class of invertebrate animals, including freshwater shrimps, crayfish, crabs, and copepods, which are mainly aquatic and have a jointed outer skeleton with two pairs of antennae and a pair of mandibles.

ctenoid scale — a rough scale bearing small spines.

cycloid scale — a smooth scale lacking small spines.

dorsal fin — a fin on the back.

esophagus — the tube carrying food from the mouth to the stomach.

family — a group of animals (or plants) containing related genera, e.g. catfish family.

fin ray — one of the stiff jointed rods supporting a fin.

fingerling — a young fish of finger length.

fleshy appendage — a triangular fleshy process above the pelvic (or pectoral) fin.

fork length — the length measured in a straight line from the front of the head (mouth closed) to the fork of the tail fin.

gall bladder — the small green sac at the base of the liver containing an alkali which neutralizes food acidity in the upper intestine.

gas bladder — the balloon-like structure in the upper part of the body cavity that helps buoy up the fish in the water. May also be used in some species, in making or receiving sounds or in breathing.

genera — plural of genus, which see.

genus — a group of animals which contains related species, e.g. the black bass genus *Micropterus* contains the largemouth and smallmouth basses.

gill arch — the bony structure supporting the gill filaments and gill rakers.

gill filaments — the red thread-like structures, a vertical row of which makes up the respiratory surface of the gill.

gill rakers — the bony projections on the inside of the gill arch, similar to teeth on a comb.

gills — the aquatic respiratory organs consisting of gill filaments on the gill arch.

heterocercal — the type of tail fin in which the upper lobe is longer than the lower and is supported by the vertebral column.

kelt — a spawned-out Atlantic salmon.

key — a series of paired numbered or lettered descriptive statements used to identify animals or plants.

kidneys — the pair of dark long excretory organs found under the backbone at the top of the body cavity.

lateral line — a sensory organ along the side, usually consisting of a tube opening through pores in the scales, which may detect currents, waves, and low frequency sounds in the water.

lingual teeth — the tongue teeth.

mandibular teeth — the teeth on the lower jaw.

maxillary — the bone forming the hind or inner part of the upper jaw.

maxillary teeth — the teeth on the maxillary bone.

molluscs — shellfish, including clams, snails and squids.

operculum — the broad plate-like structure covering the gills.

pharyngeal teeth — teeth located on bones in the back part of the mouth cavity behind the gills.

species — a kind of animal, all (or almost all) specimens of which are recognizably different from other species and which normally do not interbreed with other species.

spine — a stiff unjointed rod, often sharp, supporting and arming the fins of some fishes; or a sharp projection of a bone.

subspecies — a kind of animal usually recognizable as different from other subspecies and which occupies a definite range, but which interbreeds where it comes in contact with a related subspecies.

terrestrial — relating to the land.

testes — the male reproductive organ that produces the sperm.

total length — length measured in a straight line from the front of the head (jaws closed) to the tip of the tail fin.

trunk — the part of the body between the head and the caudal peduncle.

urinary bladder — the urine-holding sac in the body cavity near the vent.

vent — the place in front of the anal fin where the intestine, reproductive and urinary ducts open.

vomer — the bone on the midline of the roof of the mouth.

vomerine teeth — the teeth on the vomer.

A BILINGUAL CANADIAN FISHING LEXICON

A small lexicon follows of angling terms of English and French
origins that are frequently used in Canada. A very useful general
phrase book, *Travelling in Quebec: "La Belle Province,"* is distributed
by the Quebec Department of Tourism, Fish and Game. It gives English phrases and French equivalents with a simple phonetic pro-
nunciation system. For French-Canadian books on fish and fishing,
see pp. 72–75, and textual references.

bait – appât, amorce
bait fishing – pêche à l'appât, pêche à l'amorce
boat – bateau
bobber – flotteur
bottom – fond
canoe – canot
catch limit – limite de prise
crayfish – écrevisse
creel – panier de pêche
fish – poisson
fishing line – ligne, corde
fishing rod – canne à pêche
floating – flottant
fly (wet/dry) – mouche (mouillée/sèche)
fly fishing –pêche à la mouche
frog – grenouille
gaff – gaffe
guide (man) – guide
guides (rod) – anneaux
help! – au secours!
hook – hameçon
hooked – ferré
ice fishing – pêche sous la glace
insect repellent – chasse-moustique
lake – lac
landing net – épuisette, puise
leader – avançon
licence – permis
life jacket –gilet de sauvetage
lure – leurre
minnow – méné
oars – rames
outboard motor – moteur hors-bord
paddle – aviron
plug (fishing) – poisson articulé
reel – moulinet
river –rivière
rowboat – bateau à rames
sinker – plomb, poids, pesée
size limit – limite de taille, de grosseur
snap – agrafe
spinner – cuiller tournante, tourniquet
spinning – pêche au lancer léger
spoon – cuiller

sport fish — poisson de pêche sportive
still fishing — pêche sédentaire
swivel — émérillon
trolling — pêche à la traîne
waders — bottes de pêcheur (hautes)
worms — vers

Where is a good fishing spot? — A quel endroit est-ce que ça mord?
Have you had any luck? — Est-ce que ça mord?
What fly would you recommend? — Quelle mouche me conseillez-vous
    d'employer?
I would like to buy a (some) . . . — Je voudrais acheter un (des) . . .
How much is it? — Cela fait combien?
Thank you very much — Je vous remercie infiniment

INDEX

Some unofficial and less desirable common names are indexed but omitted from the text. These names are followed by the preferred name.

RESCUE BREATHING

Artificial respiration or rescue breathing may save a person's life in case of drowning. It is important to **begin artificial respiration at once,** even if there is no sign of life and **persevere** without break until life returns or a doctor has declared the patient dead.

Take the following steps:
1 Remove the victim from the water as quickly as possible. (Rescue breathing may be started while this is being done.)
2 Clear the air passages. (A sharp blow between the shoulders with the flat of the hand will often dislodge inhaled material.)
3 With victim face down and head lower than feet, press on back to expel water from lungs.
4 Turn victim onto back and lift the neck.
5 Pull the head back as far as possible by grasping chin. Hold the head back in this position. See fig. A.
6 Take a deep breath and open your mouth as wide as possible.
7 Seal your lips around the victim's mouth, as shown in fig. B. Close the victim's nose by pinching and blow air into the victim until you see the chest rise (less forcefully for children).
8 Remove mouth and let victim breathe out.
9 Repeat at least 10 times a minute (20 times a minute for children). Continue without break until life returns or a doctor has declared the victim dead.
   After first signs of life, artificial respiration should be continued for a while. When the victim is breathing without assistance, a brisk rubbing may be given to aid circulation. Then remove victim to a hospital as soon as possible.

Reference
Canada, Department of National Health and Welfare. 1963. *Resuscitation by artificial respiration.* Occupational Health Bulletin 15(7). (Ottawa, Queen's Printer). Available as an 8-page illustrated reprint.

COLOUR PLATES

PLANCHES COULEUR

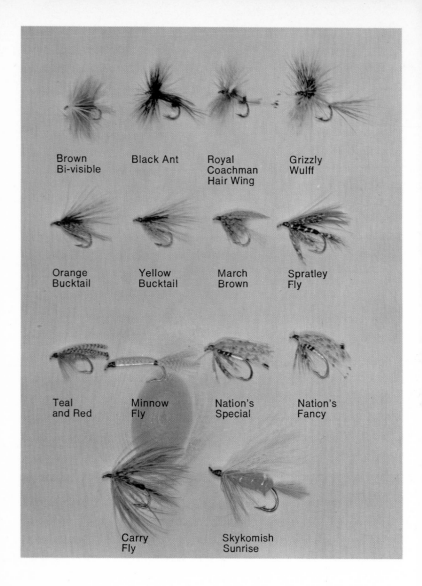

Plate 1. Fly patterns commonly used in British Columbia (tied by Mr. Joseph Jewkes, except for the Nation flies)

Planche n⁰ 1 Types de mouches populaires en Colombie-Britannique (montées par M. Joseph Jewkes, sauf les mouches Nation's Special et Nation's Fancy)

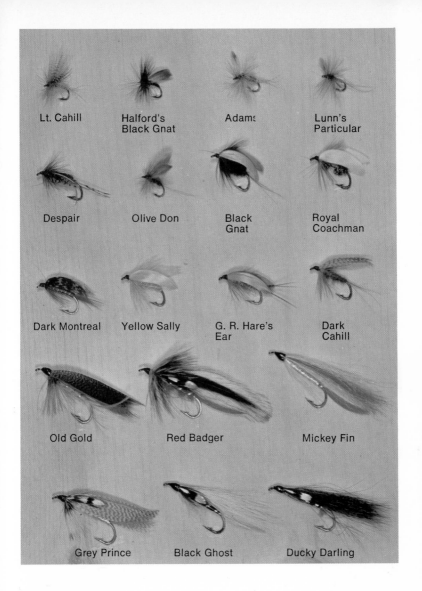

Lt. Cahill

Halford's
Black Gnat

Adams

Lunn's
Particular

Despair

Olive Don

Black
Gnat

Royal
Coachman

Dark Montreal

Yellow Sally

G. R. Hare's
Ear

Dark
Cahill

Old Gold

Red Badger

Mickey Fin

Grey Prince

Black Ghost

Ducky Darling

Plate 2. Fly patterns commonly used in Ontario (tied by Jack
Sutton)

Planche nº 2 Types de mouches populaires en Ontario (montées
par Jack Sutton)

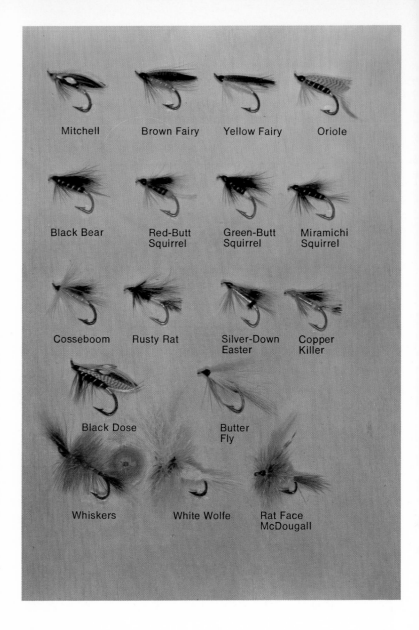

Plate 3. Salmon fly patterns commonly used in New Brunswick

Planche nº 3 Types de mouches populaires pour la pêche au saumon au Nouveau-Brunswick

A

B

C

5

A

B

C

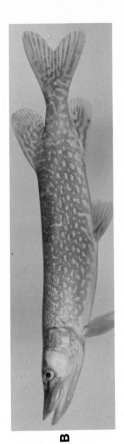

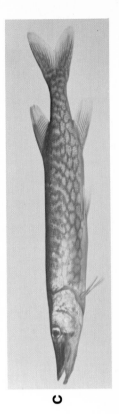

A

B

C

8

9

A

B

A

B

C

11

A

B

14

No chin barbels
Pelvics behind pectorals
Sides smooth to finger
No spiny rays in dorsal

Sturgeon family — Acipenseridae, see p. 20
- Long snout with barbels
- Mouth under and behind snout
- Rows of bony scutes, no adipose fin
- Long upper lobe of caudal fin

Mooneye family — Hiodontidae, see p. 22
- Teeth in jaws
- Fairly deep body with far-back dorsal, no adipose fin
- Ridge-like keel behind pelvics
- Long anal fin

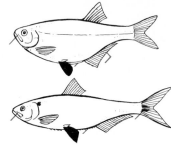

Herring family — Clupeidae, see p. 21
- No teeth in jaws
- Sharp-edged scales along belly
- Dark spot on shoulder, no adipose fin
- Flap-like scales on caudal fin

Salmon family — Salmonidae, see p. 24
- With or without moderate teeth in jaws and mouth
- Fleshy appendage above pelvic fin
- Adipose fin present
- Pelvic fin behind front of the dorsal fin

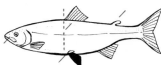

Smelt family — Osmeridae, see p. 35
- Teeth in jaws, canines on roof of mouth
- No fleshy appendage above pelvic fin
- Adipose fin present
- Pelvic fin even with or before front of dorsal fin

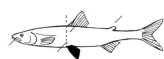

Pike family — Esocidae, see p. 36
- Long, flat snout
- Sharp-toothed jaws
- Slender body
- Far-back dorsal fin

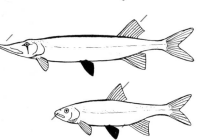

Minnow family — Cyprinidae, see p. 39
- No teeth in jaws
- Dorsal near middle of body
- No adipose fin
- Belly without sharp scales or keel

Key to Families